A NEW DIMENSION IN POLITICAL THINKING

WILLIAM J. THORBECKE

A NEW DIMENSION

IN

POLITICAL

THINKING

1965
A. W. SIJTHOFF / LEYDEN
OCEANA PUBLICATIONS / NEW YORK

Library of Congress Catalog Card Number: 64-8890
© A. W. Sijthoff's Uitgeversmaatschappij, N.V. 1965

Printed in the Netherlands

TO MY WIFE

TABLE OF CONTENTS

Table of Contents

10

Table of Contents

11

Table of Contents

PREFACE

On Easter Sunday, April 10, 1955, a French Jesuit named
Father P. Teilhard de Chardin, who lived in New York City,
suffered a stroke and died, shortly after receiving the last
rites of the Catholic Church from a hastily summoned priest.
By profession he was a palaeontologist, and of his many
books and theses not one was published during his lifetime.

After his death, his first volume entitled "The Phenomenon
of Man" appeared and was soon followed by others. Now for
nearly a decade, his theories have been discussed in many
lands, not only by scientists, in debating clubs and from
lecture platforms, but on radio, in newspapers, and in countless living-rooms among friends. In spite of his difficult style
interspersed with self-coined words to give expression to
his novel and often revolutionary ideas, people everywhere
began to struggle with their meaning which concerned in the
first place a history of the evolution of man, and in their
final analysis, a history of "Evolution" itself.

Dozens of books have appeared since dealing with the
author, his life and his heart-breaking problem, which was
to reconcile his faith and the teachings of the bible with his
scientific knowledge of man's slow emergence, during millions
of years, from the primeval mire, and the author's vision
upon a world in which thought and matter are ultimately one.
So ardent was his search for a synthesis between his duty,
his faith, and his specific discoveries, that his words stirred
many hearts and many thoughts in people who were neither
scientists nor clergymen but who found their own problems
and questions reflected in his.

Some of the books written about Teilhard and his work
branch out into other fields of science, and after nearly a
decade the flood of information pouring from the life and
works of this ascetic priest is still spreading.

Almost imperceptibly, his ideas began to infiltrate the
thinking and language of many people, much as the Austrian
Siegmund Freud's did at the turn of the century when he
threw new light into the darkness of man's subconscious

13

mind. His work and even more the opposition to some of his theses influenced scientists in other disciplines and, at the same time, made many of his scientific expressions household words used by almost everyone today. In a similar way, the priest-botanist Gregor Mendel transformed biology with his concepts of heredity and genetics, and so did Ivan Pavlov, the Russian physiologist whose research on animal behavior created a new science of manipulation of the human mind and mass psychology, and the German Albert Einstein, who not only revolutionized Isaac Newton's mechanistic physics, and some basic views on astronomy, but opened new horizons with his concept of relativity.

Like these and other scientists whose research or discoveries blazed a trail into the unknown, Teilhard was exclusively concerned with advancing knowledge and truth. Nevertheless his life's work is bound to explode many accepted views of spiritual values. He wrote as a palaeontologist, but his teachings sparked new approaches in widely diversified fields including religion.

Strangely enough, in America, Teilhard's work has had no effect comparable to that in Europe. This may partly be due to its translation * which did not do full justice to the original. In part, however, it must be attributed to the characteristics of the intelligent reading public in the United States. Their majority consists of men and women who are "doers" and "joiners" trained and conditioned to adjust their personality to their environments rather than to seek controversy, as their European counterparts do.

This author became aware of Father Teilhard's personality and work many years ago, when he headed a diplomatic mission in Peking at the time that Father Teilhard taught and excavated in China. Their roads have crossed at many points. Some of the Jesuit's close friends were, and still are, the author's too. The place where Teilhard de Chardin worked during the last years of his life happened to be right opposite the author's home in the East Sixtieth in Manhattan. He had known him, and when his first books appeared posthumously, he was among the first non-clerical men to study them and to recognize their importance. From there it was a logical undertaking to think about the application of

---

* "The Phenomenon of Man", Harper & Row, New York.

not only Teilhard's work but of the entire new Science of Evolution in his own field which is government, history and political science. Years of study and research followed and resulted in this little volume which deals with the impact of modern science on present-day political thought and world affairs.

It is not meant to attack anyone or anything. It is meant to re-think, and to make others think. It questions the validity of certain traditional ideas, it tries to shake up out-dated attitudes, and it sometimes doubts accepted concepts. It does this because nothing ever remains entirely valid under changed conditions, and because in no field of human affairs are things more apt to remain unchanged than in the intricate business of government.

Freedom, as we see it, is the right to change. Change can, and must, come by asking: "Why?" There can be no answer where no question is asked. Therefore the main objective of this book is to ask questions about the state of the world we live in, and about the impasse we are experiencing, in the hope that the readers will be stimulated to join the search for the answers.

We do not pretend to have these answers, even if we have made an attempt at certain realistic suggestions. We have no substitute to offer for dogma, myth and unquestioning belief. But we do know that the anxieties and fears of our time, the insecurity that holds the majority of mankind in its grip and jolts them into extremes, or inertia, or both, puts an obligation on every thinking person to help relieve the tortured groping among men. Only more knowledge, better education, and constructive thinking can supply a measure of such relief.

It is assumed nowadays that the thinking processes of a normal person utilize only a small percentage of man's thinking potentialities. Considering what he has achieved with this fraction of his potentialities, the future appears to hold great promise. It means that man is not near the end of his road, as is sometimes pessimistically assumed, and not likely to blow himself out of existence, but actually that he has hardly begun his mission on earth and perhaps beyond it. As his brain power will gradually develop, ever new horizons will open and undreamt of possibilities offer themselves to future generations. But even those much perfected minds

15

will be human, and there will be ever greater dangers, and new complications, and more errors and failures. There is, nevertheless, a great consolation in such a view of the future because it contains challenge and hope, and these are the essential ingredients of all progress.

We want to use those ingredients of challenge and hope, by basing this short study on a re-appraisal of world affairs today, and by adding some realistic and timely suggestions of how to escape from the present political deadlock, and to build into the future. It is but a first and halting step into the direction into which modern science points. Like any of the humane sciences, and any topic that is projected into the future it must remain speculative. It cannot but appear controversial to some people, even though it is based on science and is entirely un-doctrinarian in its approach. Whatever it is, it will be wide open to criticism and invite constructive opposition. Which is precisely what the author intended.

Chapter I

THE PRESENT BREAKTHROUGH OF SCIENCE

We are witnessing the greatest breakthrough in science of all time. Every generation invariably believes that its own time is the most revolutionary, but never in man's history have so many new discoveries in so many fields been made in such a short span of time. The results are baffling to the average person. To find a parallel to our present breakthrough, one has to go back to another advance, called the Renaissance, that began five centuries ago.

Breakthroughs result from a cumulative process of cultural experiences and social forces reaching a peak, and not from the efforts of individual men of genius. It is the other way round. When discontent with existing conditions and the desire for changes gain sufficient support, the resulting state of mind prompts the appearance of a succession of philosophers, scientists and artists who express the new ideas. No single individual can occasion a breakthrough, for if he is too far ahead of his time his views and discoveries are simply ignored. Social and cultural forces gather the necessary impetus for a breakthrough when there is a consensus that a new approach is inevitable.

The Renaissance Breakthrough

In the days preceding the Renaissance, Italian peasants, attached for the duration of their lives to the land of their feudal lord, rebelled against the immobility of their serfdom. Others, unable to stand the stifling oppression of the minuscule Italian city states, found themselves in quest of new horizons. Their imagination went out to far-away countries such as the mysterious land of Cathay. In their attempt to reach it, they hazarded themselves on oceans which, many thought, might carry them off and spill them over the brim of the world. After heroic feats of courage and determination they did not reach China, but discovered the new world.

17

The masses in Italy also revolted in another way. Smarting under the incessant reproach that having been created perfect, they spent their life in sin, they freed themselves from the hold of an intolerant and authoritarian priesthood which threatened them with purgatory and hell. In an irresistible urge to enjoy life, they rejected what to them was insufferable bigotry, and returned to the safety of the classics from Platoism to Stoicism and Epicurism. Their newly awakened aversion against superstition made them abandon alchemy and its search for the philosopher's stone, thereby inaugurating a new science of chemistry. They gave up astrology to embrace astronomy, they went in for anatomy, and re-thought many aspects of mathematics, engineering and other exact sciences. They turned to observation and inductive reasoning and paved the way for modern science. At first his return to the classics prevented the Renaissance man from formulating a new philosophy. He found his principal way of expression in the arts, in painting, sculpture and architecture, bringing a new sense of beauty and elation to the world. His primary effort to be himself guided successive generations in the difficult art of independent thinking. It would take another five hundred years before a simple, level-headed Pope, filled with love for his fellow men, eased the hold of the Roman Curia over the Catholic faithful and in his words "opened the windows of the Church to let in fresh air", but it was during the Renaissance that the decisive step toward independent thinking was made. After a time, people again lost their zest for new thoughts and their ways fell back into the old routine. It was not before World War II that a new spirit of independent thought set in, thus continuing an urge for renewal which is the most typical trait of Western civilization.

Today's Breakthrough

Our present-day breakthrough in many ways resembles that of the Renaissance. Under the threat of totalitarian aggression cultural and social forces reached a paroxism of creativity. A war for survival demanded the utmost in individual and collective resourcefulness and efficiency. If the Renaissance produced individual man, out of the modern war effort the organizational man was born, elevating the individual to a

18

new dimension by giving him the added abilities derived from teamwork. The extreme effort and concentration of energies expended in gaining victory led to unexpected inventions and discoveries, and culminated in the Promethean power which man acquired when he penetrated one of nature's deepest secrets, the structure of the atom. The discovery of atomic energy not only gave the West the "ultimate" weapon, but opened up possibilities in a whole range of other fields from technology to applied sciences, medicine, agriculture and, within the foreseeable future, genetics and meteorology, to mention only a few. In space, radio-telescopes unveiled the inconceivable distances of the universe, and radio waves suggested the existence of life on other planets. Contemporary man felt the same urge as his predecessor of the Renaissance to break out of his narrow confines. From national states he moves towards continental entities, and from there probably to a form of future world government. He strikes out into space, and for the first time in history he breaks loose from the earth and enters the infinite world of stars.

Like his forerunners he demands the right to form an opinion of his own, even if it means rejecting firmly established views, deep-rooted as they may be. His task ahead is to reconcile the latest advances of science with the myths and symbols of the past. The Renaissance discovered the scientific approach. Our time has found the key to open up entirely new worlds in physics and astronomy, biology and genetics. The salient feature of the present breakthrough is the acceleration of all development, which forces man to adjust himself to contemporary standards. The suddenness of all changes has jolted a great many accepted values and time-honored truths. Every new advance in science seems to question what looked like incontestable axioms and to lead us into a world in which all sorts of "anti-" particles and "anti-" matter lead a shadowy existence based on ephemeral hypotheses.

Difference between the Renaissance and our Time

There is a basic difference between our breakthrough and that of the Renaissance. While the latter gave people dynamism, self-confidence and "joie de vivre", all the attributes of a budding individualism, contemporary man seems to have become less certain of himself, more anxious

19

and insecure, and more inclined to seek refuge in conformism. Today the pendulum swings in the opposite direction, ushering in an age of solidarity. Various reasons cause the present uneasiness.

As already mentioned, all social and cultural forces had been concentrated upon winning the war and ridding the world of tyranny and totalitarianism. The material effort to achieve this undoubtedly raised the world's organizational level, but, during the first decade after the war, it looked as if the spiritual level would lag behind, causing an imbalance between deed and morality. Another reason for the prevailing uncertainty lies in the sudden advance of science, which defies understanding by the non-specialist and offers little anchorage. The same can be said of the support of the churches in man's quest for a way out of the impasses that beset him at every turn.

Perhaps the severest post-war trauma is caused by the clash between the use of force and the appeal to reason, between the application of new discoveries to weapons of total destruction and a budding awareness of the interdependence of mankind, between our repugnance for Communism and an urge for better understanding with all the peoples of the world, and between selfish national power politics on the one hand and efforts to create one world on the other. After an enthusiastic effort, in the flush of victory, to found a world organization under the aegis of the great powers, it soon became apparent that the attempt to submit force to law failed. Communist totalitarianism, parading in the guise of democracy, survived the war, and continued to rule in Russia and from there spread to over one third of the world's population. To make things worse, the Communists played havoc with all efforts at international understanding and openly declared their intention of dominating the world. It looked as if peace could be no more than an interlude before the outbreak of World War III. No wonder that for many, insecurity turned into fear and despair which are only recently being overcome. A series of successive crises on the international scene provided the sharpest cause for anxiety.

Chapter II

THE TROUBLED INTERNATIONAL SCENE

The trouble started in Europe. In 1914 a long period of peace came to an end. Europe was then the hub of the world. Its nations, though separated by jealous nationalism, had achieved a good deal of cohesion. Trade was free, customs duties nominal, currencies interchangeable at fixed rates, travel unrestricted and passports unknown except in Russia. In the gold standard they possessed a mechanism that regulated commerce and finance. Proud of their achievements, the nations of Europe undertook to spread the benefits of Western civilization, religion, science, justice and peace all over the world. Law and order under the Pax Britannica were enforced everywhere by the British fleet. In their vast domains they made imperialism into a fine art of blending political responsibility with commercial profit. For a while America joined in the game, but soon its deep-rooted sense of liberty prevailed and it turned away from colonialism. For the American people, freedom was more than a concept; it had become a way of life.

Various causes disturbed Europe's equilibrium. The first rumblings of the gathering storm were of a social nature. Europe's orderly progress depended on a talented and dedicated ruling class and officialdom of unquestioned integrity and strict social discipline. In the course of the Industrial Revolution, socialism, in fulfilment of its historic mission of defending the rights and economic freedom of the workers, demanded a submission to the party that was inconsistent with obedience to the ruling authority. It engendered new loyalties incompatible with the existing order and created a link between socialists, malcontents and revolutionaries of many countries, who stirred up international tensions. Another disturbing factor was the widening gap between the autocratic governments of Russia, Germany and Austria, and the British, French and other democracies. Russia's steadily pursued penetration of the Asian continent,

21

which led to the occupation of Manchuria and the Maritime
Provinces, ended in a clash with Japan in 1904. The lost
war undermined the popular respect for the Tsar and brought
a wave of revolutionary outbursts that culminated in the
Bolshevik revolution. The Austro-Hungarian empire, shaken
by the centrifugal forces generated by disgruntled Hungarians,
Czechs, Poles, Rumanians and others, tried to turn the tide
by annexations in the Balkans to the detriment of Europe's
"sick man", Turkey, only to foster new rebellions that
would lead to Archduke Franz Ferdinand's assassination in
Serajevo, one of the immediate causes of World War I.
The German empire in full ascendency around the turn of
the century, was envious of the growing colonial power of
other European nations, especially since its vainglorious
Kaiser declared that "Germany's future was on the water".
When Britain and France decided to cut op the African
continent, Germany resented being left out and decided,
whenever a favorable occasion should arise, to recoup
itself at the expense of Russia and possibly France.

The ensuing "war to end all future wars", and which the
United States joined hoping to replace the rule of force
by that of law, did nothing of the sort. The social and
political tensions which led to its outbreak became more
exacerbated. Democracy had everywhere replaced autocracy,
but the democracies proved unable to deal with postwar
problems. They were unprepared to cope with inflation and
were ignorant about the disastrous economic consequences
of collecting war debts and imposing huge reparations.
They were not capable of keeping alive the Leage of Nations,
this American-inspired first effort at world unification.

A new and insidious danger appeared. Marxism, a product
of Western thought conceived in the slums of London, Paris
and New York, brought together all revolutionaries in the
Third International which commanded loyalty over and
above that to one's country. It got its inspiration from Lenin
whose genius expressed itself in violence and hatred. Communism played havoc with organized discipline and appealed
to lawlessness and anarchy. It supported every seditious
and subversive movement. It embodied a negation of all
accepted rules of conduct and morality. It unchained a
reaction called Fascism.

Since war's end all parliamentary institutions—this

"system for gentlemen"—had been severely criticised for their ponderousness and lack of efficiency. In various countries the desire arose for a more powerful executive, directly supported by the masses and able to take rapid decisions. It was felt that only such a government could stand up to the Communist menace. However, it soon became apparent that, to succeed, such a government would have to show the same disregard for law, the same brutality and ruthlessness as the movement it wanted to fight. Fascism, and later National Socialism, had to adopt the same totalitarian methods as Communism, and also the one-party system with its total disregard for minority opinions. The more the one-party system gained in strength, the more rulers and masses became imbued with the lust for power, and the more freedom became endangered. Western democracies, unable to stem the tide, saw millions in Russia, Italy, Germany, Japan and other countries go over to the totalitarian camp. The world-wide economic depression of the thirties, an indirect aftermath of World War I, gave the totalitarians their chance to infiltrate the free world. Again tensions mounted to an unprecedented pitch and the scene was set for an explosion that threatened to wipe out all the safeguards of law and order which human society had patiently built up during the past millennia.

The disarray was heightened by the weakness of the European democracies. Instead of bolstering their defenses, they argued. When the Japanese, who were curtain raisers in bare-faced aggression, seized Manchuria, Britain declared that it had pledged itself to respect but not to defend the territorial integrity of China. When Mussolini overran Abyssinia, all Britain and France did was to propose some half-hearted, face-saving devices to the League of Nations. When Hitler sent a few battalions into the demilitarized Rhineland and two French divisions could have routed him, the French Cabinet debated. And when, after the annexation of Austria, Hitler occupied Czechoslovakia, the Western European democracies knuckled under in the Munich appeasement tragedy. Finally, when Nazism and Communism concluded their unholy Stalin-Ribbentrop pact, the war could no longer be averted. Hitler started it under favorable conditions. Germany was armed to the teeth, which could not be said of its opponents, whose morale, moreover, was low. However, when Britain regained its determination under an indomitable Churchill and Hitler took the fateful decision of falling upon his former ally, forcing Russia to join the West, and when finally the inevitable happened and the United States entered the life and death struggle for freedom, Nazism was doomed.

This war, too, ended incongruously. After Nazi totalitarianism had gone down in universal execration, its twin system, Communism, was permitted to survive and to grow in power during the years to come.

This inconsistency dominates the entire post-war world. It poses some awkward questions. Some of our soldiers asked why they had not been allowed to go on after their victory over Hitler and finish the job by overthrowing the Stalin regime which, at the time, would have been unable to resist. Apart from the question whether we alone—for our allies were exhausted—could have mustered the energy for such an immense undertaking as the defeat, occupation and re-education of Russia, there is a difference between Nazism and Communism. The former was a movement solely directed towards national self-aggrandizement, and domination of the world by the German master-race. Communism, though equally out for world domination, seeks it in the name of an abstract ideology. Even if Soviet Russia could have been defeated in the same way as Germany, the seeds of the Communist creed might not have been altogether destroyed, but might have come up again on foreign soil. This is poor comfort in view of the present Communist menace and its upsurge since the war. It raises another question. Has the advance of Communism been everywhere imposed by force or is there also a measure of voluntary adherence, and does Communism somehow fill an instinctive need, or void, which the free world cannot satisfy?

Whatever the answer, it is a fact that Stalin's annexation of Eastern Europe posed the greatest threat to peace in the post-war era, a threat that continued to weigh on the entire world. Since 1945 the Soviet Union is bent on anywhere changing the balance of power to its advantage as a means of strengthening its influence all over the world. The Kremlin started the Cold War, which is no war, but could eventually break out into a holocaust. It embarked on an ideological struggle from which there seems to be no escape and which seems to inexorably lead the world to a dead end.

While the annexation of Eastern Europe upset the old continent's balance, a more spectacular shift of power changed the equilibrium of the entire world. The European colonial powers, which at war's end found themselves stripped of most of their overseas territories, wealth and resources, lost their position of hegemony. The U.S. and U.S.S.R. emerged as the only two super-powers and achieved an undisputed military and industrial superiority. The impetus with which the scientific breakthrough shook the world gives a measure of the forces that catapulted the United States as well as the Soviet Union into their present positions. But, like a ghost from the past, the power struggle between them continues. And history teaches that whenever a struggle goes on between two major powers alone, it invariably ends with the total destruction of one. To be sure, this is a rather grim outlook in view of the weapons of mass annihilation which both sides possess.

As to the economic crises that followed World War I, the lessons of that period had not been forgotten. * Instead of demanding settlement of war debts and payment of reparations, the United States gave to friend and foe alike a help so generous as to be unprecedented in the annals of man's history. America gave to Europe grants, goods and technical assistance worth billions of dollars with the result that within a decade all of Western Europe was on its way to a major recovery. Apart from this, Washington provided help to a number of specially endangered and newly independent countries. This effort transcends normal considerations of political self-interest and bears witness to a sense of world responsibility that marks a departure from the traditional pursuit of national self-interest. Then something unexpected occurred that again raises a question. Though the United States did infinitely more for mankind than the Russians with their sometimes empty promises, Communist assistance made a deeper and more lasting impression on many people than our help.

Another important postwar change is the gradual unification of Europe. Born of the need for common defense against the

---

* Soviet Russia was the exception. It demanded large reparations from East Germany which for many years heavily weighed on its economy.

Communist danger, it freed Europe from such traditional enmities as those between France and Germany, and lessened the suspicion that often prevailed in the relations between Britain and the continent. It created a market sufficiently large for mass production and consumption, and put Europe in step with the trend of our times that reaches out for continental dimensions. It gives to the nations of Europe the inkling of a common destiny. This is all to the good, and yet Europe's integration also has certain disturbing implications. It raises the hope for recovering past political prestige and for emerging as a third power strong enough to act as arbiter between the United States and the Soviet Union. In time this could but increase international tensions by adding a new unknown to the political equation. In this way Europe promotes continental integration but thwarts world unity.

Europe's integration brings up still another problem. People ask how the prevailing tendency toward larger political entities, be they Europe's Common Market or continental federations such as the United States, Canada, Australia, the Soviet Union, or the United Arab Republic, are compatible with pride in national achievements and diversity of culture which was always considered as the keystone of Western civilization. These same people are wary of sacrificing national sovereignty to new untested blocs, a feeling shared by the United States and other federations when it comes to delegating sovereign rights to a still rudimentary organization such as the United Nations. These hesitations do not tend to ease the international atmosphere. They provoke relapses into that latent disease of our time which is exaggerated nationalism. But the greatest and most palpable danger remains Communism.

Chapter III

AN ANALYSIS OF THE
COMMUNIST DANGER AND OF COMMUNIST SUCCESSES

The Communist Danger

Communism as economic theory was conceived by Marx. Lenin made it into a militant political creed. His indictment of capitalism and its twin attendants colonialism and imperialism—couched in a cold scientific language but inspired by a searing hatred for what he called the systematic plundering of millions of enslaved workers—electrified the masses. His call for the nationalization of the means of production and the socialization of labor on a world scale found an immediate response. His dialectics gave the Communists an aggressive propaganda weapon with a choice of specious arguments.

It is common knowledge that colonialism and imperialism, as attacked by Lenin, are today mostly remnants of the past. The principal European nations voluntarily cooperated in the liquidation of their colonial empires. European imperialism, if not whole-heartedly rejected, is no longer powerful enough to be effective as the abortive Suez episode to restrain Nasser by force, clearly demonstrated. As for the United States, what it did with the Marshall Plan and subsequent foreign aid plans is precisely the opposite of imperialism.

But the masses have long memories and the systematic plunder, coercion and interference during the days of classical imperialism are not forgotten. * The militant spirit sparked

---

* Contrary to Communist allegations about American imperialism, the U.S. only dabbled in a few imperialistic ventures in the Philippines and in Latin American Republics. Nor does present investment of American capital abroad have any imperialist connotations. It is made for profit not for exploitation. Everywhere foreign administrators and technicians are trained for eventual domestic control of American originated enterprise.

by Lenin still exists among the Russian masses. It continued under Stalin, though the latter, in seeking power for his own sake, dampened their ardor. Wartime patriotism, followed by the Khrushchev regime with its greater regard for the needs of the people, revitalized their faith in the Communist movement.

Even more dangerous than Communist ideology is the opportunism of its leaders. They will seize any opportunity to further their interests at the expense of others. They will not shrink from armed aggression if they believe they can get away with it. They are out to tear apart the intricate fabric of our economy, to destroy our wealth and to place as many nations as possible under the Communist yoke. This is the grand design Lenin bequeathed to his successors.

At first Stalin was wary. He wanted to consolidate the revolution and his personal position, and to endow the Soviet Union with heavy industry, first prerequisite for a world power. He deliberately avoided becoming involved in international adventures. After a short interlude in the twenties, when he sent advisers to the Chinese Communists, he steadfastly refused them any further assistance, continuing to deal with Chiang Kai Shek until the Communist victory in 1949 left him no choice. Stalin might have continued keeping aloof, if at Teheran and Yalta the allies had not shown themselves unexpectedly accommodating. He then saw his chance, asked for and obtained in the Far East the ice-free harbor of Dairen, parts of Manchuria and the "independence" of Outer Mongolia. As Chiang had agreed to these territorial cessions, this was one more reason for Stalin to ignore the Chinese Communists and only deal with the Generalissimo. Stalin also asked for, and was given, a free hand in Eastern Europe after the war, provided that he promised to let its nations hold free elections to decide their own future. Stalin conveniently forgot his solemn promise and incorporated Poland, Rumania, Bulgaria, Albania and Hungary into the Soviet bloc under the weight of a crushing military superiority. In 1948 Czechoslovakia was also drawn behind the Iron Curtain through internal subversion.

It is one thing to profit from war-weariness and occupy half a continent, and another to hold on to it. This was one reason for Stalin to keep his armies fully mobilized while the rest of the world hastened to disarm. Stalin had another concern, America's monopoly of the atom bomb. In his eyes this could only mean that henceforth Soviet Russia and its newly acquired empire stood at the mercy of the United States. He ordered an all-out effort to catch up with our atomic superiority and surpass it. With the help of East German scientists he succeeded beyond expectation. Here lies the genesis of the Cold War. For once in possession of powerful military assets, the Kremlin embarked on a policy of nuclear threats. All the United States could do was to build a retaliatory force strong enough to deter Russia from attacking the free world. The arms race was on, and with it a period of uncertainty and danger.

Three years after the war the Communist Chinese joined the red camp and the Communist world population jumped from the original 200 million Russians to one billion, not counting Communist party members in the free world whose number, for a time, increased considerably in Italy and France, and to a lesser degree in other countries.

Encouraged by the Russian example, the Chinese Communists began a probing of their own in Korea and Vietnam which brought the northern halves of these countries behind the Bamboo Curtain, soon to be followed by the annexation of Tibet and an attack on India. The Soviet Union cast covetous eyes on Greece, Iran and Afghanistan, evinced a more than neighborly interest in Finland, made inroads in the Middle East, a traditional Western sphere of interest, and found a willing ear in some of the newly established African states of Ghana, Guinea and Mali, failed in the Congo, and established a bridgehead in the Western hemisphere in Cuba.

Both Russia and China possess in the Communist parties of other countries a potential instrument for infiltration, subversion, espionage and propaganda. These operational bases give them a considerable advantage over the free world in the deadly game of power politics. It permits them to everywhere foster trouble, prepare unexpected coups, and keep the free world constantly off balance. Had the Communists succeeded in maintaining their monolithic unity, the danger would have been still greater than it is at present. We will return to the rift between Moscow and Peking in a later chapter, and meanwhile examine the reasons for the Communist upsurge during the past fifteen years.

Communist Danger and Successes

Communist Successes

Mass Manipulations at Home

During his years of exile in Switzerland Lenin gave a good deal of thought to reactions of the masses, their cruelty, gullibility, sudden enthusiasms and docility in the face of resolute action. He became convinced that by playing on their passions and confronting them with iron determination, he would be able to bend them to his will. He applied these ideas in November, 1917, when his Bolsheviks robbed the workers of the fruits of the Kerenski revolution and grabbed all power for their small minority. Having achieved this, he was faced with the more difficult problem of how to create a new order, to continue to impose his will on the nation, and to keep the masses in check. This required more than a coup, it demanded uninterrupted manipulation of the masses. Force alone was insufficient. History of past revolutions taught that force breeds counter-force and that authority based solely on bayonets and mob violence can easily be overthrown by new bayonets and other mobs. Lenin concluded that three measures were necessary to keep the masses under control. He had to submit them to a harsh discipline and, if necessary, terror. He had to cement a strong sense of solidarity among them by creating objects of common hatred and fear. He had to instill in them a faith that each and all cooperate in a new revolutionary venture of vital importance. Let us examine these measures more closely.

Discipline and Terror

The iron discipline of the new Communist masters continued the traditions of serfdom under the feudal "knout". It became an axiomatic rule of the first thirty years of Soviet dictatorship to inflict upon the people a minimum living standard as a means of ensuring their lasting submissiveness to the regime. If the masses need all their energy to keep alive, none is left for rebellion. That is why the orthodox wing of the Communist party is still, to this day, against improvement of the living standards and unwilling to heed the call for more consumer goods. They consider an artificial impoverishment of the masses an indispensable

30

condition for maintaining the Communist system. They know
that all the authoritarian systems of the past, from Egypt five
thousand years ago to Sparta and Rome, depended upon a
system in which work was compulsory, association forbidden
and people bound to their craft. The most effective way of
keeping the people permanently down was to force fear into
the deepest recesses of their sub-conscious mind. In Russia
terror became the link with the past, the element of continuity.
It was made into an art. A Soviet manual found on the body of
a Polish officer in 1951 is revealing. It describes in minute
detail the use of terror against recalcitrant groups, how to
infiltrate them, gain their confidence and then betray them
to the police. The shock created by the execution of some
members is sufficient to unnerve others. A similar principle
is applied to individuals whose willpower is paralysed by
alternating friendliness and brutality of their police inter-
rogators. Terror is the key element in Communist brainwashing techniques.

The reason Russians still put up with all this nearly fifty
years after the revolution lies partly in the violence of
the terror itself. Under Stalin it cost thirty million un-
cooperative peasants their lives and brought millions of
others before the firing squad or into Siberian prison camps.
It also results from successful manipulation of the masses
who are told that discipline is necessary for the advancement of Communism—represented to them as a world crusade
against oppression and exploitation—for the defense of Russia
wedged between a number of imperialist foes, and for the
emulation and overtaking of capitalist prosperity.

Common Hatred and Fear

Nothing is more successful in binding the masses than hatred
and fear of a common enemy. It strengthens the sense of
oneness in the face of common danger, and it explains the
need for prolonged sacrifices and extra exertions. The
enemy, namely Western "imperialism", is the bogeyman
which justifies the Soviet government's stringent demands on
its people. Grievances against the Moscow regime are laid
at the enemy's door and he becomes the scapegoat for all that
goes wrong. American imperialism is the culprit that forces
the Soviet government to spend billions of rubles for defense

31

and space exploration as well as for education in order to keep ahead of the enemy, and thus prevents it from catering to the needs of the Russian people. In Russia, where the pay of the managerial class is considerably higher than that of the worker, though both are in the same tax bracket, the latter cannot look forward to receiving a more adequate reward for his labor. But the system is not to be blamed. It is the greed of the American "monopolistic capitalism" which is the cause of all poverty on earth. The suggestive force of such an image depends on its being endlessly repeated. The vision of the bogeyman must be drummed into the heads of the masses with dull hammer blows of ceaseless propaganda, and their attention prevented from wandering off. This is what hundreds of thousands of "agitprops" or political agitators and instructors do during millions of hours of indoctrination on or after work. Though they may be repetitious to the point of unbearable dullness, their activity serves its purpose. Soviet psychologists believe that it will continue to do so for quite some time—in fact until the day the masses, who were never taught to think for themselves, begin to do just that. By then, however, they hope that Communist dialectics will have become second nature. They may be in for some disillusionment. For already their propaganda wires have somehow gotten crossed up. The slogan of solidarity of all the workers of the world made a deeper impression on the Russian people than the image of the bogeyman, with the odd result that Americans, far from being despised, enjoy a great deal of sympathy in the Soviet Union. Or perhaps the Russian people instinctively feel that not Communist solidarity but world understanding is the demand of our time.

Cooperation in the Communist Venture

Students of history know that, in final analysis, masses are not moved by concrete aims but by abstract ideas. The most effective are those appealing to their sense of justice. The Communist citizen is told that Communism is a revolutionary enterprise for saving mankind from evil capitalist exploitation. To reach this goal requires long and painful sacrifices, but ultimately the toiling masses will find on earth the paradise that formerly was only promised in the hereafter. Then they will have equality and an equitable distribution of wealth consisting of better housing, more consumer goods and all the other amenities which are now denied to them. And if the West calls this pie-in-the-sky promises, the Soviet citizen is told that it is because democracies are jealous of the power which the Communist one-party system generates, and because they fail to understand that freedom to the Soviet man is the right to enrol under the banner of victory. In this way the Soviet masses are beguiled with a subtle mixture of fear and reassurance, pressure and hope.

So far the effort has been successful. Though there is a good deal of grumbling and discontent, the people feel that they participate in a dynamic new venture. Moreover, they derive great satisfaction from the break with the hated feudalism of the Tsarist regime. They see in the free world's pomp and opulence some reminder of their past and laugh up their sleeve about the way their government ignores diplomatic rules of conduct and its studied insolence on the international forum. * They have understanding for Communism's code of honor, which they interpret as putting the interest of the working class above a rich man's morality. There is growing sympathy and loyalty towards the regime. The average Communist is increasingly convinced that collectivism and not individualism is the trend of the future. Even in the satellite nations Communist ideology is finding greater response. To Westerners who expressed the opinion that no Communist regime could survive free elections, a Polish journalist answered that "neither Polish nationalism nor solidarity with Western Europe would be a decisive factor in such an election; if the vote turned out to be anti-Communist this would solely result from aversion to hypocrisy, lies and terror which were the outgrowths of Russia's ruthless totalitarian system and betrayal of the original Communist concepts."

In recent years Soviet achievements in space, medicine, deep-sea exploration and research in various other fields have given the regime prestige which increased the loyalty of the masses. It is as if the new dimension in Russian thinking renders the people less parochial and their outlook more global. And in their mind global and Communist problems are closely related.

---

* As when Khrushchev pounded his desk with his shoe in the United Nations.

Communist Danger and Successes

Mass Manipulation Abroad

Having succeeded in bringing the Russian people under their spell, the Soviet leadership felt the urge to achieve similar results abroad. Manipulation of the free world, however, demanded more subtle techniques than those used at home. The newly independent countries might still be won over by using the old bogey of Western colonialism and imperialism as the arch-enemy and the cause of all their frustrations; towards more sophisticated countries, and especially the United States, a different approach was required. Their will to resist the onward march of Communism had to be sapped and their self-assurance weakened. However, the peoples of the free world were used to thinking and judging for themselves and would not easily fall for the regular Communist propaganda line. To affect them would require an indirect approach and a thorough knowledge of their psychology. That was exactly what the Communists took great pains in obtaining.

In the West mass psychology had been taught at the turn of the century in Paris by Gustave Le Bon, French sociologist and author of a book entitled Mass Psychology.* After his death, interest in the subject waned until a Hitler revived it with his instinctive insight, while a Goebbels, the Nazi Minister of Propaganda, was the first to tackle it professionally. Russian scientists reinstated mass psychology as an academic discipline and Stalin spent millions of rubles on the study of how to apply the world-known biologist Ivan Petrovich Pavlov's theory of conditioned reflexes to human beings.

As a result of their research, Soviet scientists concluded that the masses are everywhere disinclined to rational thinking and ready to respond to emotional appeals. By painstaking and often ruthless experiments they discovered the kind of stimuli to be used in order to obtain certain desired reactions. They found out that the unsettling effect of alternating fear and hope-the mixture that worked so well at home-could be applied with the same success in the field of foreign relations, and that after a violent threat or

---

* "La Psychologie des Foules", at that time a widely discussed book.

34

vicious attack a subsequent let-up produced upon foreign masses a feeling of relief bordering on gratitude for the aggressor. Starting from there, the Soviet government devised a psychological shock therapy as the main instrument for conducting its foreign policy. Nikita Khrushchev became a past-master in the art. By alternating threats of nuclear annihilation with protestations of good-neighborly coexistence, he kept foreign peoples in constant suspense, straining their nerves in the hope of making them amenable to peace at almost any price. * He knew how to time his shock treatment, when to threaten, shatter hope, or frighten and when to offer the olive twig and make the friendly gesture. Both his rages and effusiveness, though seemingly natural, were deliberately planned. In all international crises during the past decade his unpredictability and the unexpectedness of his reactions added to their effectiveness. His technique proved most unsettling. By the mere fact of righting a wrong it committed, the Soviet government earned the gratitude of foreign masses who readily believed in a change of heart of the Communist leadership. Similarly the Kremlin saw to it that every relaxation is followed by new aggressive acts that dash expectations for a lasting detente. Kremnologists seek to recognize a specific design in each of these turn-abouts or to explain them by internal pressures of the army or anti-Khrushchev factions instead of recognizing them for what they are, an endless chain of aggressive acts to throw us off balance and unnerve us. In desperation our people often spoil for a fight, unaware that this is exactly what the Communists want. The extreme right seeks action, any kind of action, because they do not sufficiently rationalize the problem, accusing the government of laxity and sowing discord and suspicion and thus serving the Communist aims.

Time and again we are taken by surprise by artificially magnified incidents such as the arbitrary halting of an American convoy on its way to Berlin, the detention of an American professor on flimsy espionage charges, the refusal to return American military fliers who strayed into East-

---

* In short, he hit upon a method to produce stress which has recently been recognised in the medical world as one of the most deadly agents for man's psychological and moral disintegration.

35

Germany, etc. But not the West alone, others, too, are surprised as when Khrushchev chose his resumption of nuclear
testing in 1961 to coincide with the Belgrade conference of
uncommitted nations.* Normally one could think that this was
the time for Soviet Russia to give support to the self-styled
neutrals, upholding its image of champion of peace. But
instead of the expected gesture of understanding, the Russians chose the moment to instil fear into them, knowing
that such fear is most unsettling if unexpected, adding a
sense of insecurity on account of their miscalculation.

The Russians hit upon another device in their treatment of
foreign nations. Aware that the masses are nowhere inclined
to give much thought to what goes on in the world or to fights
between nations but are content to casually pick up some
snatches of news, they got hold of a shrewd idea. Whenever in
international disputes accusations of aggression, treaty
violations or other breaches of international law are bandied
around, the masses find it difficult to distinguish between
claim and counter-claim. They vaguely know that something
is wrong and that somewhere a danger looms. It is then that
the Communists use what could be called the method of trans-
ference of guilt. They accuse their victims of the very crimes
they perpetrate on them. Hence the constant harping by the
most imperialistic nation of our time, i.e. Soviet Russia, on
American "imperialism" and "aggression". By using this
method and branding the West as the culprit, Soviet leaders
try to evade their responsibility, confuse world opinion and
appear in the role of a righteous and unselfish nation.**

---

* The same Khrushchev who in January 1960 warned that
"should any of the states resume nuclear weapon tests ...
should any side violate its obligations, the instigators of such
violations will cover themselves with shame, and they will
be condemned by the peoples of the world".
** To mention a few examples: Khrushchev, Premier of a
country that remained fully armed after the war, accuses the
U.S. of creating a gigantic apparatus of war. Notwithstanding
Communist aggressions in Korea, Vietnam, Hungary, Tibet,
India, etc. the same Khrushchev declares that wars are chiefly
prepared by imperialists against socialist countries. After
breaking the first nuclear test ban, the Kremlin accuses the U.S.
in 1962 of blocking rearmament by their resumption of testing.

Western imperialism is given a double image. It is not only responsible for centuries of poverty and oppression, and for all adversities, disappointments and resentments of the have-nots everywhere in the world, it also represents the troublemaker who endangers the peace, the potential nuclear fiend. And this device worked. It worked when a specially harsh accusation lured under-developed countries into neutralism, or, as happened more than once in the past, one or the other of our allies hastened to come forward with proposals for a compromise after a dire threat. It worked when people of all categories, ranging from pacifists to housewives to serious parliamentarians, pressured their governments to offer concessions in order to escape impending doom, unaware that every show of fear or appeasement directly plays into the enemy's hand. It worked when in Japan professional rabblerousers caused a Presidential visit to be cancelled. And it works when hysterical crowds in some countries agitate for banning the bomb without a thought for the fate of a unilaterally disarmed free world in the face of Communist aggression. It is indeed a remarkable aspect of the Soviet psychological offensive that they get away with it. Granting that it may not be easy to overcome an initial panicky reaction when threatened with nuclear war, or to suppress a feeling of relief when the opponent suddenly reverses himself, it remains a fact that psychological manipulation can be prevented by a clear insight in its nature. It requires rational thinking and courage to resist stimuli that act on primitive instincts which put masses as well as individuals off balance. As long as nations can be swayed by emotionalism and fear, the kind of manipulation and propaganda as concocted by the Communists will remain effective. Of late there are signs that in many countries people are beginning to see through the Soviet manoeuvres.

There are other reasons for Russia's mounting influence. Its spectacular progress in science, which made the Russian masses glow with pride, also influenced foreign populations. The first Russian sputnik did more to boost Communist fame in the underdeveloped countries than years of propaganda could have achieved. Communist planning also impressed these countries. More indifferent than the West to the cost in human liberty which Communists planning demands, they see in it a shortcut to industrialization and an answer to their dreams of progress. In fact, advances in Russian industrial production and productivity are undeniable and have permitted the skipping of a number of intermediary stages which the West needed in order to reach its present economic development. To many of the less developed countries in Asia and Africa and also in Latin America, the example of Communist industrialization is tempting, and some of them are out for Russian or Chinese help in achieving similar results.

Another achievement of Soviet leadership in the psychological field and at the same time a victory of common sense over dogmatism has been to recognize that under the present stalemate of terror nuclear war has become if not an impossible, in any case a most unlikely occurrence, and therefore that their struggle with the free world must be waged with different arms. These arms are infiltration, subversion, propaganda and, above all, the unflinching effort at undermining the morale and will to resist the enemy. In this psychological war, in which they hope to achieve world domination without having recourse to armed warfare, they carefully avoid showing that they no longer believe in the possibility of nuclear war. On the contrary, they rattle their nuclear missiles at every suitable opportunity, adding nuclear blackmail to their other means of pressure.

However, their psychological warfare and peace offensive might not have become so effective, if they had not coincided with a growing desire all over the world for better understanding among nations and an awareness of global solidarity that rises as a mighty groundswell from under the turbulent waves of uncertainty. We will return to this phenomenon and to its emergence at this time and importance for the future.

Chapter IV

OUR REACTION TO COMMUNISM

Our Attitude towards Communism

American reaction to Communism is unanimous in its condemnation. Communism is wrong "per se". Undoubtedly a
strong case can be made against it. Its totalitarian character
is the exact opposite of what we consider the best form of
government. It shocks our love of freedom and thwarts the
basic principles of American government, which is to promote
and defend freedom at home and in the rest of the world. We
resent Communist mass manipulation if for no other reason
than that man is not a sum of reflexes but a being with a
conscience, a sense of freedom and a capacity to love.

Scientifically the very foundation of Communism is shaky.
Marx's prophecies did not come true. Capitalism did not lead
to ever greater extremes of wealth and poverty. Nor did
imperialism and the resulting antagonism between Western
powers break up the world economy and destroy the basis of
capitalism. On the contrary, capitalism brought a redistribution of wealth by the simple expedient of raising
wages and turning the working class into mass consumers.
Far from disintegrating, the capitalist system brought
shorter working hours, decent housing, better roads, and
many other advantages which Marx predicted would result
from Communism. Moreover, Communist parties began in
many ways to look like conspiracies for perpetuating their
power at home and extending it over other countries.
Communism disregards the rights and dignity of man, scorns
basic rules of international conduct, propagates the rule of
force and obstructs the rule of law. In spite of their protestations of peace and goodwill, Russians often sabotage
international cooperation. Their rule over the satellite
countries is more ruthless than that of the former colonial
powers over their possessions. Their secret police, though
humanized after Stalin's death, is implacable and their spy

system world embracing. These negative traits are rendered more objectionable by the fact that although Communists trick, prevaricate and bully all nations within reach of their power, theyseem to gain an increasing following in the world.

No wonder that the free countries are at a loss. Communism operates in a manner that transcends our traditional concepts of international behavior and decency. Communism has become something beyond good or bad. Since it is difficult to cope with, we rather reject it out of hand, for otherwise we might be tempted to look for something positive in Communism and, in the end, to compromise our established standards and give up the security of well-tested principles.

That is why the great majority of Americans prefer to reject Communism in toto and refuse to see that, like every human endeavour, it must also have its positive sides, that Communists may genuinely believe in their ideology and find in the conviction that they are building a new world a sense of purpose and solidarity. We forget that in their total break with the past, in which they gave up precious elements of man's heritage, they also threw overboard a number of outdated views, prejudices, and superstitions which still weigh down on the West. We think of their leadership as despotic and fail to see that it is also alert and dynamic and intent on the future. It is true that Khrushchev never has admitted his part in the Stalin era and has upheld the totalitarian character of Communism. But he mitigated the use of terror and, though out for world domination, made up his mind that it cannot be obtained through nuclear war. When he visited the United States he struck people as bright, quick on the draw, and intelligent. A man who not only talks big, but also thinks big, a man whose break with the past gave him bounce and vitality. It was Khrushchev who literally forced the world into space to open up other frontiers.

Americans prefer to think of this as an anomaly and rather agree with the view that Communism is a gigantic threat to human well-being, overlooking the fact that though Communism undoubtedly offers a threat to others, it made life less harsh for the Russian masses than it was under the Tsars. Without the Kremlin's iron rule Russian production would not have reached its present height, Russia would not have put an end to poverty, and the Soviet Union would not have become one of the world's two super powers. In their book "What We Must Know About Communism", the Over-streets remarked that "our reaction to Communism comes out of the past". But if the past should be our yardstick in judging Communism, we must remember that the Communists are not the only ones who have turned away from the past, and that the free world, too, is continuously departing from past concepts. In reality both East and West are passing through a crucible of adjustment after the violent shocks of two world wars accompanied by an unprecedented advance in science. It is increasingly felt that the existing deadlock between them can only be ended by breaking away from the hue and cry of the Cold War. If we would disengage ourselves, climb on to a hilltop and from there observe the fight, we would understand that continued attacks and counter-attacks cannot bring a solution.

A way out might be found if both sides were to re-examine their basic principles-in itself a tremendous effort-in order to discover whether a synthesis of the positive elements of both systems might be arrived at. This the free world is still wary of undertaking, and Communism even more so because of its fear of even slightly deviating from the Marxist-Leninist doctrine. The West still hesitates to view Communism as a partly abortive, partly successful venture whose leaders may, in time, be induced to change their conceptual way of thinking. Of late, something is stirring in America. In many walks of American life there are people trying to have a closer look at Russia. They feel that a change of attitude towards the Soviet Union might be advisable but are unable to pinpoint what it should consist of. In contrast to a conservative minority that continues to voice traditional anti-Communist slogans, these people, though determined to uphold freedom and avoid appeasement, are looking for a way to escape from a paralysing stalemate that compromises mankind's future. They are groping for an approach that could deliver us from the present obsession without recourse to a hot or cold war.

In their opinion there is little sense in reproaching the Communists for having sacrificed mankind's heritage in their undue haste for a change at all costs unless we, ourselves, can refute the opposite accusation of endangering our future by unduly clinging to the past. By this they do not mean that a nation should sacrifice its traditions and drift

41

from one experiment to the other. The role of traditions is to prevent just that, but not to the extent of holding on to outdated views when it is time for change and a re-orientation of political thinking. Unless we periodically review and renew our heritage, whenever changed conditions require it, they feel that it does not advance us to attack Communism for its deliberate break with the past.

The same goes for freedom. For surely it is our sacred and historic task to defend freedom everywhere, but it does not carry us much further, nor help the cause of liberty, to accuse Communism of having destroyed freedom. These same people believe that it would be better for us to formulate a new meaning of freedom, commensurate with the needs of our time, and sufficiently inspiring to awaken the Russians to a re-appraisal of their present situation. * For it is easy to forget that de-Stalinization brought some relaxation in Russia, and that collective leadership softened the worst aspects of dictatorship. Communist citizens continue to live under stringent conditions, but they never had it better than now, and therefore do not know better.

Finally these people believe that we may be too hasty in reproaching Communism of having totally sacrificed the individual to the collectivity. There are some indications that the individual is being given somewhat more attention in Soviet Russia, and not only in the managerial class. When Khrushchev declared his intention of catching up with and finally overtaking the United States economy, he needed more than commandeered performances of his labor corps. He required whole-hearted cooperation of all participants in the production process, without exception. An appeal had to be made not only to scientists, but to managers, engineers and technicians all down the line to the unskilled workers to use their personal initiative. Such an appeal necessarily implies an element of freedom and even the smallest measure of freedom can never be entirely curbed again. For a while there has also been a thaw in bureaucratic interference with literature and art, resulting in more self-assertion of authors and artists. The beginning of a realignment between individual and collectivity is taking place. We, too, are in the midst of a process of re-adjustment between the individual

---

* For a further discussion of freedom see Chapter XI page 127.

and the community. In our own world an individual can no longer keep aloof from the community. Conformism increases and society becomes more homogeneous. The individual is finding his counterpart in the community. We pride ourselves in being ruled by consensus whereas the Communists are ruled by violence. In reality we are on the verge of alienating a Negro minority with whom we no longer can establish a consensus, and in so doing we risk replacing government by consent with a police state. Many Americans are of the opinion that instead of bolstering our ego by criticizing others, we had better inspire the world by a new brand of responsible individualism which carries its appeal even across the Iron and Bamboo Curtains. An individualism aware of its responsibility to the American community and abroad, and dedicated, in the sense of our AID and Peace Corps to service all over the world.

It is a sobering thought that even if we comport ourselves according to such views, this would not notably change our relationship with Soviet Russia. It might soften the Soviet mood, it would not blunt their intent. The Cold War would go on. Something more is needed.

Red-China

In our analysis we have mostly dealt with Russian Communism because, though less militant, it is more powerful and dangerous than its Chinese counterpart. But the total Communist impact on the world cannot be gauged without understanding the nature of Chinese Communism, which in many respects differs from the Soviet brand.

It is not primarily revolutionary, for China had its revolution that overthrew the Manchu dynasty in 1911 under Sun Yat Sen. Nor is it economically inspired. At war's end China stood at the beginning of industrialization, and the country had been hardly touched by the Industrial Revolution that had shaken the Western world. Red China's Communism is nationally motivated as distinct from Soviet Communism, which began as a world revolutionary movement and only later became tinged with nationalism when this suited Stalin's personal intentions, while the war did the rest with its upsurge of patriotism.

Chinese Communism is a reaction to a century of foreign

43

subjugation. To understand this it is necessary to remember that China possesses one of the oldest civilizations. During five thousand years the people of China were convinced that the world was at their feet, that their emperor outranked all other rulers and that no other culture could stand up to theirs. When in 1840 the Opium war broke out, the incredible happened. Foreigners violated China's sovereignty, and built their own settlements where they lived under their own laws with their own police, tribunals and public services. Chinese were refused admittance into the white man's public places and parks. This started a century of humiliation during which the Chinese were pushed around, first by the Western powers and then by the Japanese. A deep hatred against the "foreign devils" seized the entire population.

When Chiang Kai Shek succeeded Sun Yat Sen, his objectives were to unify the country, subdue the semi-independent warlords and end the unequal treaties on which foreign extraterritoriality was based. In order to achieve this he leaned on the right wing of the Kuomintang party. The Communist left-wing rebelled. Chiang subdued them in pitched battles and forced them to retreat. It was then that they undertook their six thousand mile "long march" into the interior. Meanwhile Stalin withdrew his advisers and the modicum of help he had given the Chinese Communists.

In 1937 war with Japan broke out. The Communists insisted on joining the regular army to beat off the Japanese. They were given arms, which they kept for themselves and turned against Chiang when the war was over. An unfortunate American post-war effort to bring the two parties together by demanding that they open direct negotiations, made both sides lose face because it is a time-honored custom in China never to negotiate directly but only through intermediaries. In the ensuing fight the Communists finally won, but the masses had no understanding of Communist theories and only supported them because the Chiang government had become rather despotic with the passage of time.

At first there was a great deal of resistance to the collectivization of farms, to the nationalization of means of production and to the new totalitarian form of government. True, the masses acclaimed the new integrity that put an end to graft, but the Chinese were too used to freedom, and their family sense was too strong to adapt themselves to the

44

Communist regime. Mao Tse Tung broke their resistance with terror and the execution of nineteen million Chinese. When the younger generation proved more amenable to Communism and their enthusiasm waxed because they saw in Communism a means of escaping from an overbearing parental authority, and a new venture that posed challenges which only the young could meet, Mao relaxed. He spoke of a "hundred flowers", namely the variety of means by which Communism could be achieved, expecting to be applauded but not to be taken literally. The moment real opposition appeared, he reverted to even harsher tyranny, giving his Russian partners an object lesson in how to deal with obstreperous masses. His aim was to prove that China could introduce total regimentation and develop Communism according to theory, something which the Soviet Union had failed to do when it had had to give up its "agrogorods" or peasant cities. Mao pursued his policy without any regard for the people. Normally this would have increased opposition to the regime, but after the Korean war Mao could do no wrong. After the wave of criticism following upon Mao's "hundred flowers" was violently suppressed in 1957, resistance again turned into loyalty to and enthusiasm for the Communist leadership. Deep down in the hearts of the obstreperous students, dissatisfied intellectuals and disturbed party members, there was gratitude for Mao. It was thanks to him that for the first time in a century Peking had successfully defied the foreign powers. It did more, in Korea it first stopped them and then, as the Chinese were told, defeated the combined powers of the world and brought to an end a long period of national degradation and servitude. No longer need China kow-tow to any foreign country. The Communist government had accomplished the highest conceivable achievement in Chinese eyes, it had made the nation regain "face". And nothing on earth is more important to the Chinese than his "face", the image he wants others to have of him. It was this which gained Mao his unwavering popular support. His government brought back the memory of days gone by when the entire East paid tribute to China. Chinese imperialism flared up. It had never quite abated even during the century of humiliation because the overseas Chinese refused to assimilate with Malayans, Indonesians, Siamese or people of other nations where they had immigrated in large numbers, holding on to their nationality and customs and remaining a foreign element in all communities, maintaining unbreakable ties with their motherland. Today the people of China hope that their government will re-establish its hegemony over the Far East. This, more than Marxism, gives the masses a sense of participation in a great adventure.

China's reborn imperialism is certain to keep the Far East in turmoil. China's continued isolation from the rest of the world, compounded by its rift with Soviet Russia, is not conducive towards diminishing its enmity to the West. The mounting population pressure, which increases by ten million or more a year, may augment the temptation to use war as the ultimate means of extricating itself from an impossible situation. It is even imaginable that Peking would take the risk of nuclear war for enlarging its "Lebensraum", for if it lost even half of its population it still would have 350 million to stand guard over the nuclear ruins, while its enemies would have suffered an irreparable loss of manpower. Our consolation is that though Red China may before long succeed in exploding a small atom bomb, it is unlikely to be able to construct heavy bombers for its delivery, or to make hydrogen bombs or missiles. It is even questionable whether Peking really wants to attempt this and whether its aim is not to reap the incalculable propaganda value which an atomic detonation will give it. In the past the Chinese lacked the necessary know-how and perseverance to achieve important scientific and organizational feats without foreign help. This may have changed under Communism though many of their recent efforts have also fizzled out. The "great leap forward" failed and so did the communes, the new villages in which men and women were to be housed in different barracks and separated from their children, thus destroying the family and creating biological premises for the human anthill. Of late there are indications of economic consolidation, but reliable information about China is too scarce for drawing definite conclusions. A great historian, Arnold Toynbee, qualified the Chinese civilization as petrified, and though their regained military prestige may have shocked the Chinese people out of their lethargy, it is still too early to conclude that Communism can generate sufficient dynamism for making China a leading power.

It would have been quite different, had the Chinese been

able to transform Communism. For a while some Western Sinologues had the disturbing vision of Chinese, taking pride in their centuries old observance of Confucian morality, somehow chastening Communism and giving it a moral foundation. Had this occurred millions of Asiatics might have followed their example and Communism might have become a nearly invincible ideology in the East. As of today Chinese Communism presents more of a nuisance value than a real danger. But the amount of nuisance may be proportionate to the size of the country. Having regained their face, the Chinese people want more. Their hunger for prestige is not satisfied. This forces the government to keep up its threatening attitude towards the West and Taiwan, to undertake forays into India and to maintain an unbending attitude against each and all, including Soviet Russia.

All this explains the rift between a Mao who, for internal reasons, is in no position to give up his belligerent and provocative attitude towards the West, and a Khrushchev who, out of the frightful responsibility resulting from real power, arrived through a process of rationalization at the elimination of nuclear war and the pursuit of coexistence. It also explains the Russo-Chinese disagreement about the anti-Stalin campaign. For Khrushchev it meant a diminution of terror and improved living conditions for the masses, and consequently popular backing for his already considerable party support. As to Mao, who had not been consulted, it confronted him with a popular demand for higher living standards to which he could never agree. For if he fails to gain further victories and to keep up his image of invincibility, he has no other alternative than to rule by terror and to impose a minimum subsistence level. The immediate result of the rift with Soviet Russia will be a persistent effort at gaining maximum support of as many Communist and non-aligned countries as possible in the ideological struggle with Russia.

Our reaction to Chinese Communism has been military rather than political. It never went beyond the Acheson-Dulles' stage of containment. We came into direct confrontation with Red China in Korea and indirectly in Vietnam, Cambodia and Laos. Loyalty to our ally, the Chinese National Government on Taiwan kept us from giving serious consideration to the recognition of the Peking government, though it has been fifteen years in power, or to its admission to the United Nations. Long after we and our allies understood that the Cold War cannot be won by military force and that the ideological struggle with Soviet Russia has to be overcome by other means, we stubbornly continue to wage a war of containment in South Vietnam.

Chapter V

OUR DEFENSE AGAINST COMMUNISM

Our Military Defense

After the Soviet Union left no doubt about its intention of conquering the world, the United States had no other choice than to re-arm itself and its allies. For a while the United States possessed an atomic monopoly, but when the Soviet Union caught up, a totally new element cropped up in world history, the nuclear surprise attack with such terrifying possibilities as to entirely upset international relations. The prospect of a death blow in an undeclared war, dealt without warning to a nation so-to-say asleep, posed a military problem of the first magnitude. During the interwar period both France and Britain had been intellectually unable to face Hitler's semi-surprise arm, the tank. Hence the drama of an old civilization incapable of adapting itself to a new, revolutionary technique. Hence Munich and the collapse of France. But the United States, being youthful, technically efficient and fully aware of the danger, built a retaliatory force of nuclear bombers able immediately to react to any Communist surprise attack.

The Russian military threat to Europe and other parts of the world demanded more than a deterrent. The policy of containment required a cordon of allied conventional forces to forestall local wars and, after the Chinese joined the Communist bloc, the exploitation of their strategically advantageous position of forming a single, solid land mass. For this reason containment had to be global. In the beginning this demanded not only a great military but also an economic and political effort of the United States. Right after the war Western Europe was exhausted and in a kind of stupor. We had to help our allies to repair devastations and to rebuild their economy and we had to rekindle their spirit of resistance and rearm them.

Our Defense against Communism

The North Atlantic Treaty Organization * represents the first successful attempt at collective security through common defense. Making a virtue of necessity, the American, British and French divisions originally destined for the occupation of Germany were transformed into the nucleus of a protective force for Western Europe. Subsequently a ring of American bases was built around Russia's Western flank. The ring of containment was further closed by the South East Asia Treaty Organization ** and the Central Treaty Organization. *** By 1952 the United States had expanded its defense commitments to forty nations around the globe.

The United States deterrent force on the one hand and N.A.T.O., S.E.A.T.O. and C.E.N.T.O. on the other are based on different principles. The deterrent is there not to wage but to prevent a nuclear war, the other alliances to prevent or fight conventional wars. Somewhere along the line, namely in Western Europe, these principles got mixed up. Though our allies gradually increased their N.A.T.O. contributions in manpower, at the time of writing we oppose no more than sixty divisions, of which only twentyfour are at the crucial German front, to the two hundred and twenty of Soviet Russia and those of its satellites, the imbalance being made up by providing the N.A.T.O. divisions with small atomic arms of different calibers. The idea is that if the Communists should attack with overwhelming conventional forces, our side is to use gradually more and more atomic arms according to the number of divisions the enemy throws into the battle. This is called selective retaliation, or also "flexible response" with "conventional pauses", and dates from the time when our allies were unable to contribute more than a minimum to common defense. During the first decade after the war their dilemma had been to choose between rearmament and re-

---

* N.A.T.O. is an alliance between the U.S., Canada, Britain, France, West-Germany, Italy, Iceland, Norway, the Netherlands, Denmark, Belgium, Luxemburg, Portugal, Greece and Turkey.
** S.E.A.T.O. is an alliance between the U.S., Britain, France, Australia, New Zealand, Pakistan, Thailand and the Philippines.
*** C.E.N.T.O., formerly called the Bagdad Pact, is an alliance between the U.S., Britain, Turkey, Iran and Pakistan.

construction. They were also afraid of imperiling their
economy, aware that any depression might provide a fertile
breeding ground for Communist subversion. Having been
used to seeing the United States defray the major part of
their defense expenditure, they accepted small atomic arms
as a welcome alternative to the costly and unpopular raising
of more manpower. At first the United States also hesitated
to augment its conventional forces. A further increase of
its defense costs —which gradually crept up to 55 billion
dollars a year—could endanger the free world's economy.
For nothing would suit the Communists better than to see
the United States and its allies bleed themselves white by
keeping up an arms' race with a totalitarian regime that has
greater facility in manipulating its economy than the free
world.

But, ingenious as it might be, the idea of compensating an
inferiority in conventional forces by small atomic arms is
not likely to work under all conditions. It may succeed, as
in fact it did, in preventing a large-scale attack by Soviet
conventional forces. As John Foster Dulles put it "our
nuclear force is powerful enough to deter the Communists
from waging any major conventional war, because they know
that it will lead to nuclear war, the West being sure to resort
to the use of nuclear arms to defend itself". However, in
qualifying his statement by using the term "major" war,
Dulles left open the question what is to happen if Communists
use conventional forces for achieving limited objectives or
for tactical purposes. The question is not whether we will
use nuclear arms if the Soviets attempt to overrun Western
Europe with a hundred or more conventionally armed divisions. We will without any doubt. The question is what
happens if, for example, Soviet intransigence leads to an
armed clash on the Autobahn to Berlin, the fighting spreads,
and both sides send in re-inforcements? N.A.T.O. might
engage a division or two, the Russians even more, and finally
we could find ourselves greatly outnumbered by superior
forces. The presence of the West is at stake in Berlin. We
are likely before using atomic arms to use the "hot line" to
Moscow to make it clear that unless the fighting stops we
have no other alternative. The Russians in turn, may refrain
because a system of graduated atomic defense may well
escalate into nuclear war. However, if neglotiations ensue

51

we will not have the advantage, which we had in the Cuba affair, of overwhelmingly superior conventional forces nearby, but this time the Soviets will have it. And this will weigh heavily against the West's obtaining acceptable terms. For it will be negotiating from weakness, which would be unnecessary if with the help of our allies we would, once and for all, put an end to Soviet superiority in conventional manpower.

In other parts of the world there is even less cause for using nuclear arms. No statesman is likely to incur this fateful responsibility unless the most vital interests of his country are at stake. During the Indo-China war when, according to French Foreign Minister, George Bidault, Dulles twice offered the use of American atom bombs for the defense of Diem Bien-phu; the offer was declined because of its danger of leading to general atomic war. Neither were nuclear arms used in Korea or South Vietnam.

The logical solution of how to protect the free world from limited Communist attacks with conventional forces is to increase the combined conventional force of N.A.T.O. The alliance needs more conventional troops for two reasons. In the first place, in order to beat off any limited conventional attack without the use of nuclear arms and the danger of escalation and, secondly, because without parity in conventional forces our negotiating position 'vis-a-vis' the Communists remains weak. In 1962 American conventional forces were increased by fifty per cent, and this gave Washington a reason for urging the allies to equally increase their N.A.T.O. divisions.* It is a fact that since Europe's remarkable economic recovery the reasons that militated against higher military budgets no longer exist. Today Western Europe is fully able to raise more divisions, and it is mostly the hope that the United States will continue defraying most of the costs that keeps them from doing it. In France the situation is different. There President De Gaulle holds back on his N.A.T.O. commitments in order to obtain greater political and military say in all affairs concerning the alliance.

For a while it looked as if Europe would inevitably become the battleground, if the two super-powers were to clash.

---

* In the same year General Maxwell D. Taylor who all along opposed our main dependence on nuclear arms, became Chairman of the Combined Chiefs of Staff.

This made some European nations uneasy. Though the consensus was that the United States would keep its commitment that any attack on N.A.T.O. would be considered as an attack on itself, some doubt was voiced as to whether in the case of a local fray, and notwithstanding the danger of its escalation into a hot war, the United States would unleash a nuclear holocaust and risk the annihilation of its large cities and the loss of millions of American lives. This gave President De Gaulle an argument for his 'force de frappe'. He already had misgivings about Britain's separate nuclear force, which it maintained for defense of the Commonwealth but which he ascribed to a favored position resulting from Britain's special relationship with the United States. And there was still another consideration, nationalism, the grandeur of a France which deserved and therefore demanded a place equal to that of the United States and Britain in the councils of the West, and a leading position in Europe. Finally there was the matter of prestige. As a French commentator formulated it: "Western Europe cannot resign itself to the permanent status of protected country". As soon as prestige comes into play, reason gives way, and a perfectly logical issue becomes confused.

As rationalized in this country, the basic elements of the N.A.T.O. defenses are: (1) that a strong nuclear force is necessary as a deterrent, (2) that as long as this force is sufficiently strong, it is not likely to be used and operates as a kind of collective insurance, (3) that the building of additional nuclear forces is therefore an unnecessary and costly duplication unless Western unity falls apart—which is tantamount to Communist victory, (4) that today all N.A.T.O. allies are able to and should increase their conventional forces in order to reach parity with Russia in this field, too. Western Europe lies geographically within Soviet military range and only by restoring the conventional power balance can it deliver the free world from incessant Russian military pressure. If it is likely that our retaliatory force will deter the Soviets from waging nuclear war, it does not necessarily prevent them from undertaking conventional attacks or a military squeeze play. Recent history shows that wherever the free world possesses superiority in conventional arms, confrontation with Communist armed power turned out to our advantage as in Greece, Lebanon, the Straits of Taiwan and Cuba. * Where our conventional forces have been weaker, as in Korea, Berlin and Vietnam, the situation has remained a source of potential danger.

Under present circumstances even a partial pullback of American forces from Germany could have undesirable consequences. It would be an invitation for West European nations to rely on themselves and to create national nuclear defenses, withdrawing funds necessary for their conventional forces and, by sheer multiplication of nuclear forces, increasing the overall danger of nuclear war. Until such time when there will be a truly international force for keeping the peace, continuation of the American deterrent, coupled to greatly strengthened conventional N.A.T.O. forces, seems the most logical solution. Europe can trust the United States. And it must trust us, for without America there is no adequate defense against Communist military power. A French contribution to a European nuclear force can never take the place of a contribution to Europe's conventional forces. Defense against Communism is a matter of global, not national concern.

With the appearance of the intercontinental ballistc missiles the U.S. and U.S.S.R. could attack each other directly and the overall picture changed. An eventual battleground shifted from Europe to both these countries. In the grim international poker game which asked for ever higher antis, Khrushchev came out, in 1961, with a hundred megaton nuclear bomb, more than five thousand times the power of the Hiroshima bomb, with the "reassuring" remark that he still had heavier ones among his chips. In order to be capable of delivering such heavy bombs, the Russians steadily perfected their high thrust space boosters and payloads. Our military experts, whose duty it is to prepare for any eventuality, and who already had obtained huge appropriations for an anti-missile warning system and anti-missile missiles, now insisted on a military space program of manned and armed satellites. A controversy arose about giving such a program priority over the N.A.S.A. program for putting a man

---

* In Cuba the Soviet Union obviously wanted to put pressure on the U.S. in view of the forthcoming Berlin negotiations. They possibly introduced their missiles without the intention of using them. This could explain why, in their eyes, these missives were "defensive" weapons.

on the moon which, for a time, was considered the best way of re-establishing American prestige after Russia's striking success with Sputnik.

Meanwhile another change occurred. The arms' race reached a point that practically precluded any attempt, from whatever side, of waging nuclear war. From retaliatory, the United States nuclear force became indeed a deterrent. Provided the United States keeps it up-to-date, and barring miscalculations, nuclear war becomes more and more improbable. It is the United States deterrent that made the Kremlin renounce nuclear war and embark on the Cold War. Those who still may doubt that the Soviets have given up nuclear war in earnest, should bear in mind that the Kremlin's irrevocable decision not to provoke such a war was made at the tremendous cost of a break with Red China and the resulting disintegration of the Communist monolithic bloc.

The war continues but is fought with psychological weapons. And even here still another change took place. When President Kennedy made his proposal for a joint moon venture with Russia, partly in order to find a spectacular form of co-operation and partly for reasons of economy, Premier Khrushchev declared that the Soviet Union was temporarily not in the race. Thus in the psychological war, too, a possible cause of friction may, for the time being, have been eliminated.

Our Psychological Defense

Against an opponent who puts his main effort into psychological warfare, no military defense, however perfect, can be sufficient without a corresponding psychological defense. The latter aims at strengthening civilian morale, countering enemy propaganda and stimulating the right attitude towards the opponent.

People of the free world are being currently informed about Communist psychological tactics. This is the best way of immunizing them against subversive manipulations. Forewarned is fore-armed. The Cold War is not waged with guns, tanks, bombs and missiles, but with insidious means that may prove more deadly in the end. It is more than a war of nerves, it aims at destroying the opponent's courage, his moral resilience and faith in himself and his institutions. Communist technique is not much different from that used by Madison Avenue experts who learned to play on man's subconscious mind. The difference is that the latter influence the individual's taste by making him react to certain stimuli, while the Communists attempt to weaken the collective spirit of resistance. With their brainwashing at a distance Communists cannot hope to win the masses of the free world over to their creed as they did with a few of the American prisoners of war in Korea. However, they do succeed, by their alternation of fear and reassurance, in first angering them, then plunging them into uncertainty, and finally into indifference.

Guidance about the opponent's intentions is more efficacious than counter-propaganda. In many respects our propaganda turned out to be less effective than expected. Answering Soviet propaganda, blast for blast, leaves the initiative to them. It keeps Western propaganda on the level of recriminations instead of introducing ideas that transcend the Cold War. The free world could deprive Communist propaganda of its most important psychological weapon by convincing the American and allied peoples that the Kremlin may be rattling bombs and missiles, but that it has no more intention than we have of embarking on nuclear war. Once this thought has been firmly implanted in their minds, the West's negotiating position will automatically improve. Washington and our allies might be concerned that public opinion would thereupon oppose the present huge defense expenditures; this can be avoided by a clear-cut explanation of their imperative need as a means of preventing war. As President Kennedy said in his inaugural address: "For only if our arms are sufficient beyond doubt can we be certain beyond doubt that they will never be employed".

Though the outbreak of nuclear war is highly improbable since the two main opponents have reached a stalemate of terror, it would be unrealistic to say that it is absolutely impossible. There always remains a danger of miscalculation. As long as both sides are able to rationalize the situation, this will not occur because the free world will not take the initiative in starting such a war and neither will the Soviets on account of our superiority in bombers, guided missiles and nuclear submarines. But in our very superiority lies an element of danger, the danger that it leads to fear. And fear is the foremost reason for miscalculation. In Communist countries there exists an undercurrent of fear of the United States. It began with Stalin. We were the first to drop the bomb and during the time that we had an atomic monopoly Stalin felt more than uncertain. Dulles' liberation slogans and brinkmanship were not reassuring to the Kremlin. The Russians were afraid, and fear never was a good counsellor. All great historians from Sallust on, and even a Napoleon in his St. Helena memoirs, insist that fear engenders war. It was fear of Russian extension in the Balkans that drove Hitler into his fateful war with the Soviet Union. Today part of the Communist party is not sure that the United States may not one day resort to a preventive war, and if they and the army should at a certain moment become panic stricken, this could lead to an explosion. The moral of this is that we need a deterrent but must use it wisely and had better leave bomb rattling and threats to the opponent. To inspire the Communists with respect for our power is right, to increase fear among them inadvisable.

There is another approach to our psychological defense, which is to take the psychological offensive. But then indirectly, namely by changing the climate of thinking in the Communist countries. Not by propaganda alone but by physical penetration of the Iron Curtain whenever there is an opportunity, as through trade, scientific and cultural exchange, tourism, etc. Once the Communists feel no longer isolated from the rest of the world, this is bound to influence their thinking and to strengthen a subconscious solidarity with other nations and especially with the United States in whom the Russian people have a lingering confidence. Psychological defense against China raises a similar problem. Because Red China is still intent on war and aggression against the West we steadfastly have ignored Peking. But would it not be wiser to encourage contacts with China, to pierce the Bamboo Curtain and to make the people and leading cadres aware of different outlooks on life and other political concepts? The choice is difficult as long as it remains a matter of expediency and not of basic considerations.

Summarizing the problem of our defense against Communism, we conclude that nuclear war is unlikely, provided that we keep up our deterrent. We are, however, in the midst of another kind of war, fought by psychological means which,

57

at any time, can be reinforced by conventional attacks and local wars. If all free nations became fully aware of this and were prepared to accept the hardships and privations which wars normally impose, they would close the conventional defense gap in order to stand unassailable in the psychological war. They would also make a major effort at wresting the initiative from the Communists and putting an end to the Cold War. The question is how to achieve this without appeasement or retreat under fire, real or psychological.

This is the main problem that faces our statesmen, for the pressure is mounting for liberating the world from the ideological stalemate. Though love of freedom lives in the hearts of all men, today an appeal to it no longer carries the force it did in the past. Perhaps because, for the time being, freedom is being identified with the individual and the nation, while it is neither the individual nor the nation but mankind's collective destiny which touches man's deepest anxiety.

Something different is expected from our statesmen, a new vision and a new approach in a new spirit of understanding. Something in the very direction in which —as the world belatedly recognized—the late President Kennedy had begun to move. Such an approach requires patience and circumspection on account of the many difficulties which a new and unconventional endeavor is certain to encounter everywhere.

Chapter VI

THE ENIGMA OF MODERN SCIENCE

After our analysis of the anxiety caused everywhere by the Communist danger, and before going into the task that awaits contemporary statesmen, we still have to examine another factor that contributes to modern man's loss of equanimity. Caught unaware by the forward leap of science, he sees his efforts to catch up with it frustrated by science's transformation from a source of unwavering truth into a pool of fluctuating approximations. To those who probe a little deeper into the matter, it seems that after prying into nature's remotest secrets and harnessing the use of atomic energy for further extending its domination over the earth, science readies itself for breaking away from the confines of this planet. In the effort to reach out towards the new secrets of space, it is as if everywhere new and unforeseen perspectives arise.

At the threshold of the space age there are men who feel a kind of exhilaration and the urge to overcome a number of conventional attitudes of the past and to rely on rational thinking alone. It is not that they object to metaphysics. On the contrary, their philosophy of science contains an element of deep religiosity, free from dogma and superstition. They refuse to lean too heavily on the past and pin their hope on the future, convinced that this future largely depends on the further improvement of man's mind.

Others, and they are in the majority, undergo a different reaction. To them science seems to have suddenly reached a bewildering impasse. To understand what has happened, it is necessary to go back to Isaac Newton. His mechanistic theory of physics gave man the secure feeling that the universe is governed by immutable rules which he had finally come to understand. It permitted him to predict, for all time, all movements in the universe, or so at least it seemed. During two hundred years nothing happened to change this view. Then, around the turn of the century, mechanistic physics ran into difficulties. A first doubt was raised in 1900 by Max Planck's quantum theory, according to which radiant energy is not an unbroken stream but consists of discontinuous groups of particles called quanta. Planck did not arrive at this conclusion through observation, but through a theoretical computation showing that the amount of energy carried by each group, divided by its frequency, leaves in every case the same small remainder called Planck's quantum. But as this belonged to the realm of mathematics, the mechanistic fiction of science could be upheld. The rift came when a young patent clerk in Bern, Albert Einstein, applied the quantum theory to light, proving that light, too, travels through space in separate quanta. As a result there are at present two theories on light, one that it consists of quanta, and another that it consists of waves, because certain phenomena of light can only be explained by a wave theory. This became the first serious inroad into mechanistic physics and its explanation of everything by mechanical formulas.

The next anomaly appeared when it was proven that the ether, which was an indispensable element in the Newtonian set-up, does not exist. Two American scientists, Michelson and Morley, made a meticulous experiment based on the assumption that if there was an ether, a light beam travelling with the earth against the ether stream would be slower than one travelling in the opposite direction. The experiment proved beyond doubt that the velocity of the light beam remains constant and thus—unless one is prepared to deny the earth's motion—that there is no ether.

This was a blow to Newtonian physics. It was followed by an even more telling blow resulting from Einstein's Theory of General Relativity with its postulate of the indivisibility of the space-time continuum, which put an end to the neatly compartmented concepts of space and time. Finally Einstein's famous equation $E = MC^2$, meaning that energy equals mass multiplied by the square of the velocity of light, or that mass and energy are somehow interchangeable, brought down with a crash the majestic Newtonian edifice with its separate halls for matter and energy. The assumption, at first theoretical, that matter and energy are interchangeable, that matter can shed its mass and become radiation and energy, and that energy can congeal into mass, became reality when the first atom bomb exploded transforming matter into energy, and heralding in a new scientific age. *

The final death-blow to mechanistic physics was given by Einstein's Unified Field Theory, which postulates that the theoretical relationships involved in gravitational and electromagnetic fields are the same. This amounts to a denial of the Newtonian concept of gravitation as a force of attraction that permeates the entire universe, emanating from all particles of matter and acting on all of them across the boundless emptiness of space. To Einstein such an interpretation of gravitational force was an illusion. He considers gravitation to be a deflection from inertia, i.e. the tendency to go on moving in the same direction unless acted upon by some outside force. He believes the movements of stars and planets to be determined by physical conditions prevailing around these celestial bodies such as bumps caused by electro-magnetic fields which they encounter and which deflect them from their normal course determined by inertia.

Such clarification of scientific thinking can only be welcomed, even if it upsets a great many established principles. But things become awkward the moment science is no longer able to suggest satisfactory alternatives to the principles it discards. In many fields it is no exaggeration to say that the farther science penetrates into the nature of things, the more contradictory and confusing its conclusions become. Growing insight into the atom shows that matter mostly consists of empty space. Take any hard object such as a table, which consists of a countless number of atoms. Each of these atoms contains a nucleus around which electrons move as planets around the sun. The distance that separates each electron from the nucleus is fifty thousand times as large as the space the electron itself occupies. Consequently the atom nearly entirely consists of empty space. As Arthur Koestler * * put it, a room with a few specks of dust floating in the air is overcrowded compared to this emptiness of the atom. And a table consisting of millions of such "empty"

---

* In an atomic (fission) bomb onetenth of one per cent of the mass is converted into energy, in the hydrogen (fission) bomb seventenths of one per cent.
* * "The Sleepwalkers" by Arthur Koestler.

atoms makes on us the impression of being absolutely solid on account of the coarseness of our senses. The atom offers another contradiction in connection with the movement of its electrons, which cannot be traced. Electrons in their circling around the nucleus jump from one orbit into another without traversing the intervening space, simultaneously passing from one state of energy into another. The only conclusion to be drawn from this is that electrons dematerialize somewhere and rematerialize somewhere else. It seems that the closer matter is scrutinized, the more it vanishes.

Not only is today's scientist of two minds as to whether matter consists of particles or of waves, but also is he unable to escape from the impasse that as an observer he is caught in the field of his observation. This point can best be illustrated by the following examples of observations in the micro- and macro-cosmos.

In their microscopic observation of atoms scientists are not sure at all that the act of observation does not affect changes in the observed. In order to find out how an electron comports itself within the atom, a quantum of light has to be directed on it. It so happens that this quantum of light has an effect on the electron, for otherwise it would not become visible. This poses the question whether the electron's movement which we observe is spontaneous or results from the impact of the light quantum. This example illustrates what scientists call the principle of indeterminacy, meaning that there are things that cannot be known. Unable to establish identities in the microcosmos, scientists had to be satisfied with establishing probabilities. Like the actuary in insurance or the forecaster of traffic accidents, he has obtained a great degree of precision in establishing these probabilities. This method permits the discovery of laws in nature even if they cannot be precisely observed.

In the macrocosmos, observation presents difficulties of another order. Our inability to gauge the immensity of the universe, even with the most modern radio telescopes, or to measure cosmic forces, makes every observation hypothetical. Today a number of different theories are advanced to explain the phenomenon that galaxies seem to move away from the observer at the speed of light, as indicated by the changes in their spectrum. The Explosion theory explains that this results from an explosion of extremely dense matter some nine or ten billion years ago. It finds a certain corroboration in the fact that by measuring their nuclear processes, it was discovered that the oldest stars indeed originated some eight or nine billion years ago. But a strong argument against the theory is that the very force which caused the genesis of the galaxies will one day be exhausted, leaving the universe devoid of any matter and energy, and this is not in keeping with the rhythm and polarity inherent to the process of evolution. The Expansion-Contraction theory postulates that after the galaxies cool off, their expansion will be followed by contraction bringing the universe back, after billions of years, to its starting point when matter again becomes so dense that it causes another explosion, and the entire process is renewed. Though this theory does recognize an alternating rhythm it raises another objection. The endless process of oscillating between creation and annihilation, which it anticipates, is at variance with the irreversibility of evolution, the generally accepted fact that evolution proceeds into one direction without ever running backwards again. And so still another theory, the Steady State theory, proclaims that if an all-embracing observation of the cosmos is impossible, scientists have to fall back on philosophic assumptions. One of these is the existence of a continuous creation of matter in the universe, where galaxies are born as the result of a cooling off process of matter which is everywhere to be found in space in a stage of extreme heat. However, as the average density in space, according to Einstein, must be constant, the creation of new galaxies must either be accompanied by an expansion of the universe or by the annihilation of existing galaxies. This alternative possibility is a moot point. It is generally assumed that continuous creation of matter postulates an expanding universe, steady annihilation of matter a contracting universe. And admittedly the universe cannot simultaneously expand and contract. In the macrocosmos, too, contradiction and uncertainty prevail.

And so science continues to disclose one contradiction after the other. This goes so far that scientists now consider waves constituting matter as mere "waves of probability". Reality has become an approximation, or a dream, and the universe is no longer the precise machine of a Newton but a fleeting thought. Then there is the shadow-like presence of anti-neutrons, or of anti-matter that may have no existence at all. In this growing confusion the danger is far from imaginary that science is becoming imprisoned in its own closed system and, defining everything in its specific symbols and jargon, is in the end unable to find a way out of the maze of its own creation. There is another danger. Should science finally despair of causality, being unable to find a law for the behavior of the atom or other phenomena, and conclude that the only rule in the universe is the law of chance, then mankind would not only have reached a scientific but also a moral impasse.

All those who, during the past centuries, rejected the supernatural and "a priori" superstition, looked to science for an answer. They hoped that man's destiny could, at least partly, be determined without recourse to pre-ordained laws unfathomable to logical understanding. At present, however, science has not succeeded in establishing such rational rules and man's destiny appears to be linked up with unpredictable atoms, non-existing anti-matter and waves of mere probability. And so with science unable to explain anything, the word "meaning" itself is becoming meaningless, moral values become figments of imagination, and a philosophy of existentionalism with its stress on personal desires in a purposeless world, justified.

It is hardly surprising that in such a world a great many people are at a loss. In contrast to the men, mentioned at the beginning of this chapter, who believe that man's mind will in the end be able to cope with present confusion and who rely on rational thinking and are forward looking, there are many others who seek security in the past and refuse to think about new political or spiritual purposes. Still others, who see their civilization with its achievements and expectations on the verge of disappearing into a mental chaos, only retain a desire for material gain and selfish progress.

It is in such a world, where science no longer offers the support of logic and basic laws and in which a new ideology derides existing political convictions and traditions, that statesmen are called upon to re-establish order in benumbed minds and peace among stirred-up passions.

Chapter VII

THE TASK OF TODAY'S STATESMEN

Today's Statesmen and the Cold War

In the foreign field the historic duty of statesmen was to defend the national interests, maintain the status quo and safeguard the peace. Today's statesmen have the same tasks to which a formidable new one has been added, namely to stand up to an ideological struggle which is spreading all over the world and which threatens it with universal decline of all moral standards. In the past national interests had precedence over all other considerations, the "status quo" served to uphold existing sovereign rights, and peace to safeguard the national integrity. Today none of these objectives can any longer be viewed from the national point of view; all must be seen from their global context. In the nuclear age peace has become indivisible. It is no longer peace for one or more nations, it is peace for the whole world that is at stake. If anywhere nuclear war should break out, all nations will be involved. The foremost task of contemporary statesmen is therefore to keep the world at peace, to seek adjustments where leading powers clash, to respect tacitly recognized "status quo's" and, most difficult of all, to bring about such living conditions all over the world as to prevent misery, oppression and mismanagement from creating anywhere a climate of despair from which war can spring.

In the course of this century it looked as if nationalism with its absolute sovereign rights might give way to closer cooperation between nations under a code of international law. Statesmen had the vision of a world rising above nationalism and evolving towards supra-national institutions which, one day, might grow into a world government. They hoped that with patience and perseverance virulent nationalism with its accompaniment of strife and war could be overcome and the rule of force change into a rule of law.

The emergence of the present ideological struggle changed

65

all this. The free world had to resign itself to the fact that the United Nations, on which so much hope had been placed, was powerless to stem the Communist tide and that only a return to power politics and military alliances could save freedom. Western Europe had to be protected and the intrusion of Communism into Latin America, Africa, the Near, Middle and Far East barred. It was the Communist threat that also forced back on the free world the concept of spheres of influence which now became zones to which Western countries had access but from which Communism had to be excluded.

Such concepts are familiar to Communists, for power and influence are natural vehicles of their foreign policy. In the past Russia's power ambitions had always been aimed at extending their hold over Siberia deep into the Far East, and immediately after the war they made their coup in Eastern Europe. But on other continents they felt, at the time that the Cold War started, like newcomers, like young industrial concerns facing established competitors who already had carved up all markets among themselves. In their eyes the existing international order merely served the purpose of protecting Western vested interests — the United Nations, the International Court and other World Organizations being packed with pro-Western elements. So they made up their mind to fight the existing order, and its protective shield of international laws, as a matter of principle and by all available means.

Totalitarian Communism itself cannot suffer the slightest inroad on its sovereign rights lest its hold on its own people be weakened and its freedom to interfere in the affairs of others hampered. Neither can it desist from creating uninterrupted international tensions lest the rest of the world regain its composure. This is ample reason for sabotaging the United Nations, as the more than hundred vetos used by the Soviet Union in the Security Council prove. The ideological chasm between East and West is too deep, their respective views on international law and the sanctity of treaties too divergent to permit any realistic hope for their cooperation in building a world ruled by international institutions. There is at present no other way left to Western statesmen than direct dealings with Communist states in order to prevent headlong collisions.

66

The result is a power struggle, pure and simple, waged partly on the physical level, partly for men's minds. In a previous chapter we dealt with the military and psychological defense measures our statesmen were forced to take. The question is what else they can do and, in the first place, which Communist weaknesses they can exploit. We already saw that such weakness hardly exists in the military field, though China is definitely weaker than Soviet Russia by its lack of nuclear weapons and missiles, which cannot even be made up for by the two and a half million men they keep under arms. Communist weaknesses do lie in agriculture and, to a lesser degree, in industry. In China each farmer feeds three persons, himself and two others, in Soviet Russia a farmer feeds seven persons, in the United States thirty, and America, moreover, has a large yearly surplus * while China suffers from periodical famine and Russia had to buy millions of tons of wheat in the West as a result of bureaucratic over-organization coupled with the farmers' recalcitrance. It might seem a matter of simple logic to exploit this weakness and to bring home to Moscow, that inveterated champion of the use of force in international relations, that a loss of power to Russia is a gain of power to the United States. The same logic seems to demand that if Russia is unable to meet certain industrial demands, there is no reason why we should help them out with Western goods. If Western statesmen nevertheless acquiesced in sales of wheat and industrial products, it was not only for reasons of profit or for redressing an unfavorable balance of payments. Their decision was also motivated by an undercurrent of solidarity with the Russian people. Others argued that such humanitarian considerations should not enter into political decisions. Here then we have a typical example of one of these fateful decisions with which Western statesmen are faced, and which are so hard to rationalize for lack of a clearly defined philosophy to fall back upon.

---

* In fairness it should be noted that American intensive cultivation shows a disadvantage to Europe and Asia, where thousands of years of organic manuring by peasants have created a thick layer of fertile soil, whereas in parts of the U.S. topsoil became so thin and volatile as to be at the mercy of any heavy storm, changing arable land into a dust bowl.

There are other Communist weaknesses which Western statesmen are able to turn to our advantage. When competition with the United States forced Khrushchev to inject a measure of freedom among Russian workers, he thereby introduced the most dangerous of all ferments to a totalitarian society. Yet the West can do nothing to accelerate its effect. The process must follow its course, and foreign intervention could only slow it down.

The same goes for the budding bourgeoisification in Russia, reminiscent of the gradual change from socialism's revolutionary militancy to Labor's respectability. Transition from Communist "sans-culottes" to bureaucratic managers is only beginning, but it provokes impulses towards, in Communist eyes, "dangerous" class associations. Just as the military produced an "esprit de corps" that does not necessarily concur with Communist party views, the managerial class may develop ideas that do not tally with the party's aims and, for example, may favor increased foreign trade. Here Western statesmen can indirectly help by encouraging such trade, except in strategic goods. Foreign trade is an important means of increasing contact with the Russian people and its leading class. It can stimulate their imagination and independent thinking, things incompatible with the collective system. Such contacts can also bring into focus the image of a more affluent way of life and raise the question in the Communist mind why, in view of their other achievements, better rationalization could not also have protected them from a great deal of unnecessary hardship.

Still another Communist weakness is their sensitivity to unforeseen changes across their borders. This became noticeable at the time of the Hungarian uprising, when a nation always described as friendly to the Russian people turned overnight into a fierce enemy. Hence the Kremlin's savage intervention and its ludicrous assertion that the Hungarian revolt was a fascist machination, by which it hoped to reassure its people about the sudden turn-about of a nation which they had been led to believe was staunchly Communist. This kind of sensitivity can be exploited by the West's refusal to recognize the incorporation of the European satellites in the Soviet empire, or the partition of Germany, as established facts. As regards China, the rise of a Communism "à outrance" in that country with its three thousand miles of common border with Russia, had an even greater impact on the Soviet people. It evoked the deep concern that the fate of the Chinese peasants and workers might one day befall them.

By far the greatest weakness in the Communist world is caused by the rift between the Soviet Union and China. It broke the monolithic force of Communism. It planted seeds of disintegration that may disrupt the entire Communist movement. It may upset the world's equilibrium by causing war between Russia and China. At times the leaders of the Kremlin may be haunted by the spectre of hungry Chinese hordes descending upon the planes of Siberia. Should history repeat itself and the exploits of a Ghengis Khan or Tamerlane be renewed, the Soviet Union would have to come to terms with the West in order to protect its rear. These are only speculations, but they open new perspectives to Western statesmen in their appreciation of Communism. Before it would come to an armed outbreak between them, both Russia and China are likely to make strenuous efforts at healing the break. The advantage of presenting a common front still outweighs whatever differences they have. Communist realism demands Communist solidarity and an eventual alliance of the Soviet Union with the West, or its adherence to the Community of European nations could only be envisaged as a last-ditch defense. But history has seen stranger re-groupings. In any case, Western statesmen are right to keep aloof from the internecine Communist fight lest any effort at exacerbating it bring both sides nearer together again.

Western statesmen realize that they can do little to intervene or to influence closed Communist societies. They concentrate their efforts on the rest of the world by highlighting the basic differences between freedom and Communism. At times, however, they encounter the alarming phenomenon that in parts of the world people are no longer able to understand why freedom and Communism are diametrically opposed. A number of so-called unaligned nations look at the clash between freedom and collectivism as a power struggle in which they do not want to become involved.

Neutralism *

To them the Cold War is a selfish fight for world hegemony, ruthlessly conducted with little concern for the rights and interests of other nations. In Europe the question is asked why we always react so sharply to every kind of Communist challenge. Even among our allies some people find our "intransigence" towards the Soviet Union difficult to understand. Others are of the opinion that in the case of nuclear war their nations will be the first victims and that, whatever the outcome, they will be at the mercy of the super-powers, and so they conclude that neutralism is the best course. They forget that it is only our and our allies' determination that can prevent war, and that the fate of all free nations would be sealed the moment the United States shows the slightest inclination for appeasement. As Benjamin Franklin said: "Those who give up essential liberty to purchase a little temporary safety, deserve neither liberty nor safety". Theirs is the neutralism of despair.

There are other kinds of neutralism. There is emotional neutralism, prompted by the humanitarian desire to protect mankind against the horrors of war, and culminating in a crusade for unilateral disarmament. It contains a veiled criticism of American materialism which, in England, is compounded with a nostalgic urge to revive British grandeur in the form of moral leadership aimed at banning the bomb. This neutralism does not stand up to reason, because unilateral elimination of the means of waging war cannot eradicate the causes of war, and only increases the temptation to engage in war for those who remain fully armed.

Then there is the neutralism of impartiality, of nations which feel called upon to act as arbiter of mediator, and at the same time are glad to hide their indecision and lack of courage behind this expedient. Finally there is the neutralism of the newly independent countries. The latter are exclusively concerned with their independence. To them freedom is freedom from colonialism, and political liberty is of little

---

* Neutralism is a state of mind not to be confused with neutrality which is a legal status, either self-imposed, as in the case of Switzerland, or imposed by others, as in the case of Austria.

avail to them. To those African countries which are still near to tribal rule, democracy is something new and hard to understand. Being recently liberated from colonialism, they fight shy of power politics. They accept help but do not want to be under obligation. Theirs is the neutralism of selfdefense.

Among our allies there are those who find that instead of being intransigent we should be more aggressive in our attitude towards Communism. Bonn, especially under former Chancellor Adenauer, showed concern whenever Washington started direct negotiations or even conversations with Moscow. There is no easy manoeuvring in the ideological struggle for Western statesmen.

Mirage and Reality

It is far more difficult to find a solution to the Cold War. After years of mounting tension, a still vague but nevertheless persistent clamor arises all over the world for better global understanding and greater interdependence. It has caught the ear of many a statesman. Attempts to crystallize this general desire remained, however, tentative and hesitant, probably because a rational explanation of such an upsurge for world solidarity still eludes us. What efforts were made remained mostly one-sided and uncoordinated. The United States' show of global responsibility as expressed in its massive international assistance, was often looked upon by the world at large as an effort to keep its allies in shape and to win unaligned countries to its side. Russia's foreign help and its peace campaign were ascribed to ulterior motives by all except genuine Communists.

Statesmen who undertook a serious effort at bridging the gap between the free and Communist worlds, ran into powerful opposition, in the United States as well as in the Soviet Union.

In the United States a strident anti-Communist propaganda hardened public opinion to the point of rejecting any objectivity. Under the influence of emotionalism and oversimplification it classifies its statesmen only under the heading of "hard" or "soft" towards Communism. In the past McCarthyism was overcome by the self-control and aloofness of President Eisenhower and others, but at present it often seems as if both parties are vying with each other in their protestations of anti-Communism. Such hackneyed slogans as the liberation of Eastern Europe, armed invasion of Cuba or the breaking off of diplomatic relations with the Soviet Union still find a ready response among certain people. However, cold logic and a detached view of the world situation lead but to the one conclusion that to expect a Communist capitulation is unrealistic and that Communism is there to stay. Neither is it likely to yield to force or to be overthrown by internal revolution. As time goes by, however great their hardships, Communists show a growing solidarity with their regime and the Communist cause. Even in the satellite countries anti-Communist feeling is diminishing. Better and cheap housing, paid education and all medical expenses have something to do with it, but the main reason may have been best expressed by a young East-German intellectual: "We do not believe in Communism, but neither in capitalism, we have no ideology to fight for, so why revolt?"

As already remarked, it is this lack of understanding of freedom which makes the task of Western statesmen difficult. They, and especially American statesmen, are dedicated to the defense of freedom and the dignity of man all over the world. Freedom is the mainspring of Western political thinking, the one unquestionable issue for which free men are willing to make the supreme sacrifice. And now freedom is apparently losing some of its appeal. Is it because America should have given freedom a new content more in agreement with the needs of our time? However this may be, the conviction of all who believe in liberty, that it is the highest good and represents man's most sacred heritage, makes it impossible for Western statesmen to follow any other road than that of leading freedom to victory. They will not swerve from it nor compromise with it.

Communist statesmen, on the other hand, though less positively inclined and rather stressing their historic fight against capitalism and imperialism, also have an active faith in collectivism, which they relentlessly pursue. They, too, ran into opposition when they tried for a detente in the Cold War. Khrushchev's policy of co-existence was violently attacked in China, but also criticized by the Russian army and the diehards of the party.

The harsh reality is that Communism lives or dies by the acceptance or rejection of a collectivist dream and that our democracies find their irrevocable justification in the difficult art of governing men in freedom. The West is dedicated to freedom under self-discipline, Communism to the collective effort enforced from above. The West is democratic and the East totalitarian. Neither East nor West are politically able to give up their ideology. Both opponents see in the spread of their system over the world the only possible outcome of their struggle. And so things have come to a dead end. Without a solution in sight, the fight is to continue and only reason can prevent it from breaking out into suicidal folly. That is what American and Soviet statesmen have made up their minds to prevent. But all the Soviet Union can offer is co-existence, which is passive and therefore a poor substitute for any positive action towards a solution, while all the free world can promise is not to go to war provided that Communism stays within its present boundaries and does not spread. But this would condemn the world to a static condition which is contrary to the laws of nature. The future of the world hangs on a tenuous thread unless its statesmen can transform the present uncertain truce into an active co-operation. Even then all efforts will remain mere expedients unless both parties achieve the seemingly impossible, namely composing their ideological differences.

Once the leaders of the U.S. and U.S.S.R. make up their mind to avoid nuclear war, this establishes a point of convergence between them over and across the existing ideological differences. Notwithstanding the opposition which each is likely to encounter in his country, they may succeed in finally surmounting the ideological barrier. For they must understand that as long as each opponent continues to think exclusively from his own premise, each of them will be always right and the other always wrong in each other's eyes, and the future will remain dark. It must occur to them that each side should make an effort at enlarging his own basic thinking in order to arrive somehow at a common frame of reference.* Unless they make the effort the world will again

---

* When Einstein enlarged on Newton's laws and created new laws, he broke through an existing frame of reference and brought new notions of reality. In the ideological struggle it is up to the genius of statesmen to come up with new ideas that can correlate two opposite frames of reference.

and again slide back into new and fiercer periods of cold war.

Statesmen Have no Time to Think

To compose an ideological strife requires abstract thinking. Contemporary statesmen have little time for this. Especially a President of the United States, who is constitutionally head of state, chief executive and the man responsible for the conduct of foreign affairs, all in one. A so heavily burdened official cannot be expected to find the time necessary for thinking out what amounts to a synthesis between freedom and collectivism. And yet there lies the only lasting solution for ending the Cold War. To be sure, changes in the Soviet Union and the United States may eventually bring it to an end, but what the world needs is not to wait for a favorable turn of fate, but for man's own efforts to ward off, as soon as possible, the danger that reason may give way to passion and war engulf us.

Neither President nor statesmen can know all the facts. These must be studied by officials, experts and, sometimes, outsiders who then submit a number of solutions for the current problems. It has been said that all a President or statesman has to do is to choose one of them. This may be correct for routine decisions, but if it comes to hammering out a general line of foreign policy, this becomes an individual creation. Particularly at a time in history when such a line has to be redrawn, existing premises abandoned and a new course entered. Such a break in continuity can only be conceived by one man. Changes in history admittedly result from social and cultural forces and are therefore in a way predetermined, but it needs a man of vision to discern and reveal them to his contemporaries.

However, Anglo-Saxons are pragmatists rather than abstract thinkers, and Americans are moreover doers rather than visionaries. Yet, whenever circumstances demand it, a man is likely to arise with sufficient perception and dynamism to change the course of history.

It becomes increasingly clear that in the United States a public opinion is evolving which wants to change the fight against Communism into a fight for something. It recognizes that wat the world needs is a common purpose that transcends existing suspicion, fear and preconceived ideas. A

74

concept that grips the imagination and envisions a new equilibrium to which all nations can rally, the Communists included. An effort to break away from a routine Cold War enmity and to "be of our age", i.e. to subordinate ideological differences to the needs of mankind, to its physical survival, to its mental adaptation to the space age and above all to the necessary education and research for facing the tremendous challenge of our time. A determination to establish peace with the clear understanding that peace requires more power, more intelligence and more ingenuity than war.

The question is where, in the midst of their daily pre-occupations and relentless pressures, can statesmen find the basic notions that can inspire such a new course.*

Chapter VIII

WHERE TO FIND THE INSPIRATION FOR A NEW COURSE

Political Science Fails Us

The first thing to do is to rationalize the existing situation. To find an answer to the question why after the common effort at ridding the world from Nazism, Communism's appeal grew, freedom lost some of its appeal and why after various efforts of introducing the rule of law in international relations, power politics still prevail. Why after the effort which brought about an unprecedented breakthrough in science, mankind witnesses a recurrence of violence, aggression and ruthlessness. Is Communism solely responsible for all this or are these the symptoms of a crisis that befell the whole human race? A crisis arising from an unbalance between a sudden advance in science and technology and our moral progress. Why otherwise should the world be dazed by an ideological struggle, cowed by impending nuclear self-destruction, haunted by the desire to end a bad dream, and yet unable to rid itself of a mass of slogans, intolerance, hatred and fanaticism? And this while at the same time people pray for peace and understanding, and everywhere the stronger and wealthier nations offer succor to less prosperous countries. These contradictions, because they are world-wide, point at something more serious than the usual troubles which precede periodic re-adjustments in history. This mass paralysis on the one hand, and outpouring of sympathy on the other, suggest a crisis in mankind's development. Again the question arises where to look for a cure and possible solution.

A political scientist would be inclined to turn to his own field for an indication of how to overcome the Cold War and its demoralizing effect on the world. Demoralization which touches all nations. For it is this kind of corroding uncertainty, this wavering between hope and despair, which saps their vitality, reduces their courage and makes them lose interest in everything except material security. It is doubtful

76

whether Political Science can suggest any remedy. Political Science deals with the theory of government, relationships between states, rules of international law and international institutions. It is mostly interested in the past and is not equipped to make prognoses. It does not operate, like the economic and social sciences, on the basis of trends or relevant variables. It never made a point of distinguishing between variables, or of finding out which of several future alternatives is likely to occur. Political Science is not tuned to anticipating the political future of nations and still less the future development of mankind.

And yet the direction in which human society is going to develop is our basic problem. What we want to know is whether there is a gradual shift from the individual to the collectivity as suggested by the mounting homogeneity of mankind and the desire for solidarity. Are we heading for a totalisation of the human race and is man's ultimate destiny a fate similar to that of the social insects? Is Communism, with its tendency to restrict the role of the individual to specific social functions and to reduce his initiative, a prelude to the monotony and robotism of a human beehive or termitary? Or are we right in supposing that the human experiment cannot be compared with that of the social insects for the simple reason that the latter's size was too small to ever develop anything like man's brain, and that the human mind will make it possible to arrive at a society in which both individual and collectivity play a part of equal importance? Finally we ask ourselves if, in our pre-occupation with the individual, we of the free world may have failed to recognize that the collectivity is more than an aggregate of individuals, that it may be a phenomenon of equal importance to that of the individual.

Should it be possible to discover an acceptable hypothesis about specific rules that control the evolution of mankind, differing from those that define the evolution of other species including the social insects, then mankind's future would no longer be a matter of chance; it would be progressing according to a logical pattern.

The answer to many of the questions we raised depends on the existence of such a pattern. Western man's inability to see the forest of mankind beyond the trees of individualism and nationalism may be due to his insufficient understanding of the role which humanity plays as a whole. The same goes for the Westerner's dismay that freedom lost some of its magic and his inability to restore it. This he may regain from the moment that he understands that man does not aimlessly drift, but develops according to a plan in which freedom has its place. In this way he may overcome his feelings of frustration and mental stagnation, and reach out for a new purpose.

If Political Science is unable to give a lead in these weighty problems, there are a number of mutually related sciences which, though less in the limelight than the exact sciences, nevertheless shared in the general scientific breakthrough and which can help us in our quest. Biologists were the first to provide answers to some of our questions, but it was the modern science of evolution, based on findings of archaeology, paleontology and other closely related disciplines, which came forward with a number of hypotheses, scientific theories and new philosophical views that can provide statesmen of the world with new basic approaches.

Here a word of caution is called for. The subject matter is highly abstract. I have tried to reduce it to its simplest expression, but it still demands a good deal of concentration to be understood. Aware that my fellow Americans do not as a rule hold with abstractions and generalizations, I nevertheless draw their attention to them, because experience has taught me that, with very few exceptions, men are able to understand almost anything and because they will find ample reward in their effort.

Changing Views on Evolution

To grasp the problem of our time it is necessary to go to the heart of the matter. And the heart of the matter is man. Too long have we given our undivided attention to history, forgetting about the more gripping and revealing story of man. To understand man, knowledge of his past is essential. His past and future form an unbroken line called man's evolution. The modern science of evolution collects as much knowledge and as many data as possible from man's past. Reaching back to his very origins and extrapolating from the facts it thus gathers, it makes a projection of man's future development. The concept of evolution has greatly changed since the days of Charles Darwin who was the first to have the intuition and perception of a continuous process of development, but who is also remembered for his fiercely opposed theory that man descends from the primates. This, by the way, is an over-simplification, his postulate being that man and primate have a common ancestor. The outcry against Darwin's theory of a century ago has in the meantime abated, though there are still people today believing that the world was created in the year 4004 B.C.* They refuse to bow to the evidence that man's past reaches back to the Pliocene, as recently proven by Louis Leaky's find in the Olduvai Gorge of Tanganyika. This specimen, which possesses a larger braincase and teeth more human than those of the primates and which was found amidst tools, is one million seven hundred thousand years old. This brings man's evolution more in harmony with the slower development of preceding animal species and with biologic evolution in general.

Since the days of Darwin, scientists have reached the conclusion that man, although he is a product of evolution, stands apart from all other species. Harvard's paleontologist George Gaylord Simpson expressed it as follows: "Man is not just another animal. He is unique in extraordinarily significant ways, being the only organism with a true language. This makes him the only animal who can store knowledge and pass it on beyond individual memory." Other scientists reached similar conclusions.

Sir Julian Huxley, whose grandfather, the biologist Thomas Huxley, defended Darwin's theory, also insists on man's unique position. He points out that since the early Pleistocene, one million years ago, whereas the previously dominant groups of animals have diminished through widespread extinction, man has multiplied, extended his range over the earth and adapted himself to various ways of living ranging from roaming nomad to sedentary farmer, from slave to free man, from doer to thinker and inventor, from discoverer to space man, etc. Unlike former dominant types which evolved into hundreds or thousands of separate species, man's variety was achieved within the limits of a single species. In animals, evolution is divergent and occurs by isolation of groups which

---

* A fact reminiscent of a debate in the Netherlands Parliament during the first decade of this century about the question whether or not the serpent did speak in the Garden of Eden.

become progressively different in their genetic characteristics. In man, after an initial divergence between the various
races, the different branches came together again maintaining
mankind as a single species.

According to Huxley, man represents since the Pleistocene
the only avenue of progress. All other efforts of nature led
into blind alleys and only the path that man has taken seems
to lead indefinitely onwards. In the past all animal species
turned limbs and jaws into specialized, and therefore limiting,
instruments. Man alone kept his freedom of action because
man is the only creature to create instruments without
identifying himself with them. Man learned to fly without
becoming a bird, to dive under the waves without having to
become a fish, and to use millions of instruments in order to
dominate his environment without the need of any structural
change within himself. Man who, unlike other creatures, is
prepared to mate at any time, has a rate of fertility which is
enormous and offers the possibility of more rapid selective
changes than found in wild animal species.

Man's individual development is extremely slow. From
birth to sexual maturity takes a quarter of his normal life-
span instead of one eighth to one twelfth in other animals.
J. B. S. Haldane, another biologist of repute, remarks in this
connection that animal litters cause an acute struggle for
existence in the prenatal period and that such intra-uterine
situation puts a premium on the rapidity of growth of such
animals, who therefore miss man's slow maturing. Man's
slow development is necessary for the evolution of rational
thought and for the acquisition of those skills which he
absorbs from and contributes to the accumulated knowledge
of the species.

Conceptual thought could only have developed in a mam-
malian stock which normally brings forth one young at birth.
To arrive at this conceptual way of thinking—and his accumulated traditions—man needed many favorable factors.
Among his ancestors, the primates were arboreal, which
helped develop sight and thumb. This in turn gave them a
new knowledge about objects and their manipulation. These
primates were gregarious, leading to the development of
speech, which could never have evolved in a solitary type.
And speech is the physical basis of conceptual thought. These
are the reasons which Huxley gives to explain the emergence

of man. To make the step from sub-human to human, primates had to descend on to the ground, acquire an erect posture and convert their forearms into manipulating hands. *

On the basis of these premises, man learned to think, to speak and to use tools. He did more. His flexibility and complexity became incomparably greater than those of any other creature. He overcame the rigidity of instinct. His plasticity of mind permits him to relate any activity and thought in whatever field. This gives him the possibility of a unified mental life, though it also creates conflicts within him. Man has a unique capacity for abstraction but also for synthesis, especially in the fields of pure mathematics, music, art, religion and romantic love. In conclusion, Huxley calls man the sole representative of life in the progressive aspect of evolution and its sole trustee for future advance. Through his inventiveness man has found methods of bringing forth progress that are less dilatory, less wasteful and less cruel than those of natural selection, the only ones available to lower organisms. There may be other creatures endowed with reason, purpose and inspiration, but we do not know of them. The only thing we know at present is the uniqueness of man and consequently the unique future that awaits him. We may add that man is just beginning to realise his role in evolution, which from an object makes him into a participant with increasing possibilities for guiding his own destiny, provided that the human race finds the way to pool its energies and to create a spiritual force whose achievements may indeed be limitless.

This raises the question of how man is going to develop the collective organization of the species, and whether he is likely to continue in the direction of free associations, such as tribes, races, nations, civilizations, religions, etc. with traditions and cultures of their own, or whether he is headed for an all-embracing integration of the species.

---

* In this they followed the example of the extinct dinosaur species whose Iguanodon had an erect posture thanks to the counterpoise of a huge tail, and also short arms and claw-like hands with five fingers.

Inspiration for a New Course

Man's Future Society

A foremost biologist, Caryl P. Haskins, deals with this problem in his book "Of Societies and Men". He compares the view that man, being unique, his evolution necessarily will have to be a unique occurrence in nature, different from anything in the past, with the opinion, presently shared by Communist philosophers, that man's integration into a totalitarian society is the logical result of evolutionary laws as exemplified by the tightly organized communities of the social insects.

Haskins, who is a social philosopher as well as a biologist, compares the integrated insect societies such as the termitary, the ant hill, the beehive and the so-called "colonies" of the Portuguese man-of-war, with a totalitarian society and concludes that what they have in common is the absolute subordination of the individual to the interests of the community and rigorous restriction of the individual's personality to well defined functional activities.

In his analysis of the question of whether man's evolution is likely to follow the way of the higher insects, he mentions three conditions necessary for the foundation of an integrated insect society, namely: (1) that the founding members, such as the termite, bee, or ant queens, must attain considerable longevity so that they may survive many broods of their descendants, (2) that the founding members must be immensely fecund, capable of giving rise to tens of thousands of progeny and (3) that the reproductive members of the tightly integrated society must comprise a decided minority of the total population, and the rest must be non-reproductive. He adds that man, or any warm-blooded vertebrate for that matter, is biologically incapable of fulfilling these conditions.

Compared to that of the insects, man's evolution is extraordinarily dynamic. He achieved in less than ten thousand years what took the highest social insects fifty million years. Within three hundred generations since the beginning of civilization man has surpassed the experiment made by ten million generations since the appearance of the Eocene ant. This, by the way, proves that the acceleration in creative and inventive thinking which characterizes the present phase of man's evolution advances in something like a geometric progression as compared to preceding periods of evolution.

Another argument against the likelihood of man's development gravitating towards an integrated society is that all through evolution natural selection is based on the concept of individuality. So much so that once the integrated insect society or the "colony" had been definitely constituted, it assumed some of the characteristics of the individual and from then on natural selection occurred between rather than within social insect groups. * In the case of man, however, the human race remained one single species and never divided into a number of integrative societies, with the result that selection cannot otherwise continue than among individuals, which requires man's individuation and not his integration. That seems to dispose of the danger of man moving in the direction of an integrated society, leaving intact his traditional family and associative ties. However, Haskins sees the danger elsewhere. He is concerned about the future of what he calls man's "cultural society". He uses this term to describe the extraordinary complex of ideas originating from man's brain and their continuous exchange with millions of others. He thinks that "this complex may, without too much fancifulness, be regarded as a being in itself, a living, changing, adaptive organism with an independent existence and evolution of its own". Here Haskins reached the same conclusion at which Teilhard de Chardin—to whom we will refer later—arrived when he spoke of a "common thinking organism" to which he gives the name of "noosphere" or sphere of the mind, in contrast to the biosphere or sphere of life.

Haskins attributes to this "cultural society" an emerging personality of its own that exists in close, if uneasy, partnership with the ancient biological family association with which it is, in fact, in desperate disharmony. Such a collective organism strives, by its very nature, at integration. It is, therefore, more comparable to the societies of higher social insects than to the primarily associative biological forms of man. Haskins further asserts that new ideas, which he calls the genes of the new "cultural society", do not need to be

---

* In a remarkable book "The Life of the Termites" the South-African biologist Marais considers the termitary as a single living organism with the queen as its brain and the termites its cells receiving commands sent out by the central brain via their antennas.

biologically inherited in order to be transmitted throughout the civilization which they affect. They are propagated by imitation and learning. A mutation in the form of new ideas will rapidly spread because the "cultural society" as a thinking organism no longer possesses the genetic barriers of slow and uncertain heredity * which protects an associative society from becoming integrated. In other words, if the incredibly slow biological mutation of the past is replaced by a new, constantly accelerating, mutation of the mind, the "cultural society" lacks the former defense mechanism of time and is more likely to slide into integration. He recognizes in the "cultural society" an already existing tendency towards specialization and concentration on one's specific work. This will steadily increase, leaving overall thinking to a minority. In many professions and industrial enterprises selection of personnel is already today largely made on the basis of cultural attributes especially suitable to that particular group. This stimulates selection of ideas according to their timeliness and immediate usefulness, a method likely to facilitate thought control.

All this reveals a tendency towards a "socialization" of mankind that may lead to some measure of integrated thinking. There is, however, a difference between "socialization"—or as we would prefer calling it, solidarization—and integration. Solidarity means that each individual feels one with the community and the community one with every individual with the result that everyone is at liberty to freely express his thoughts. Integration is the exact opposite, for it would change the common thought-organism into a regimented thinking machine and transform the individual's perception into a functional operation that would only benefit a leading minority.

In addition to this basic objection to Haskin's conclusion that thought mutations lead to thought control, there are also some specific counter-arguments against that thesis. The more untrammeled the flow of thinking becomes and the greater the opportunity for exchanging ideas, the more difficult it is to force these ideas into traditional grooves and the more they will represent rational perceptions rather

---

* For the problem of heredity see also Chapter IX, page 95 and Chapter X, page 106.

than imposed opinions. Because new ideas spread with increasing rapidity, they will more and more accelerate the clash of opinions and thus contribute to clear and independent thinking.

Granted that specialized thinking is on the increase in the Communist world and even in the West, as exemplified by the fact that the average employee of thousands of "big business" enterprises uses the same arguments and slogans as his fellows, and that scientists and universities use a jargon only understandable to experts, fear that this may lead to integrated thinking in the free world is not born out by other facts. In an increasing number of modern enterprises, qualification for executive leadership no longer consists in a special business mentality or in the art of getting along with others, but in creative intelligence. The same goes for politics because gradually more careers are made, not by toeing the party line, but by showing originality of thought. And a number of outstanding scientists make it a point to write in clear, popularly understandable language. It can be said that in our society, intelligence, imagination and creative thinking are increasingly in demand for leading positions. These qualifications, in themselves, prevent a too great specialization of functional thinking by stimulating interest in general issues and competition in overall thinking. The resulting kind of leadership is vastly different from that invested in a totalitarian hierarchy which, by definition, is infallible, free from basic criticism and not exposed to debates on a footing of equality. Such hierarchy, based on power, is indeed foredoomed to integration.

As long as a sufficient margin of private initiative is maintained, the danger of totalitarian thought mechanization is remote. As long as individualism and human dignity are respected, no thought organism is likely to become integrated. The same goes for all forms of modern communications. As long as newspapers, radio, television, etc. continue to be free, the establishment of an integrated society is unthinkable.

Solidarization in freedom leads to convergence, not to integration. That is the point Haskins overlooked. Convergence of thought leads to sharper thinking and this, in turn, to a further perfectioning of the human brain. And thus man's evolution advances towards an ever deeper awareness and not towards the kind of functional thinking that typifies the social insects, and for that matter the totalitarian systems. Once the common thinking organism reaches a certain acceleration, new ideas will spout at such a fast pace that none will have time to congeal into dogma or ideology that would last for more than a fleeting moment in the course of evolution. A constant flow of new ideas will create elasticity in the common pool of thinking that makes for incessant change, and as change is the essence of life, for increasing vitality.

In the past the written word with its depersonalized objectivity, had considerably less impact than today's spoken word over the radio or the visual presentation of the speaker on the television screen. The more varied the views thus presented, the less people will be subject to indoctrination in a single direction. And, giving free rein to our fantasy, we might even anticipate a further innovation whereby not only the words of the speaker and his image are recorded but also the thoughts behind his words. This would indeed put an end to any mass manipulation, without which no totalitarian thought integration can be established.

Chapter IX

THE THESIS OF TEILHARD DE CHARDIN

Having examined the views of some modern biologists on man and humanity, we now turn to another scientist whose original outlook and bold hypotheses on evolution highlight the breakthrough of this branch of science, and whose breadth of vision and warmth of understanding bring order to man's mental disarray. Pierre Teilhard de Chardin possessed one of those lucid minds able to grasp the nature of the present crisis and to guide man back into the right evolutionary track. His vision of man's evolution is so sweeping that it transcends and leaves far behind such ideological disputes as to the merit of free or collective societies, and offers elements for a synthesis that can lead mankind to an undreamt future. His words hold a promise which can restore to man faith in himself, give to the world a new hope and purpose, and thus provide a basis for solving our political problem.

The Man

Teilhard de Chardin (1881-1955) was a French paleontologist of world reputation. In his early years he studied geology and philosophy, taught physics and later studied prehistory and archaeology. From these days dated his friendship with the Abbe Henri Breuil, another famous archaeologist. * His collaboration in the excavations at Chu Ku Tien near Peking,

---

* The author became acquainted with Teilhard in Peking and Breuil in South Africa. The former struck him as a brilliant, imaginative and methodical scientist and philosopher, the latter as a combination of sensitive artist and original thinker, both deeply human and with an extraordinary intuition for their work. Coincidentally, and though neither scientist nor Catholic, the author is also friendly with a third Jesuit priest, de Saguez de Breuvery, high U.N. official and Teilhard's confessor shortly before his death.

which led to the discovery of the "Peking Man", 475,000 years old, established him as an authority in the science of man's origin and evolution. Much later he investigated the discoveries of Broom, Dart and Robinson in South Africa concerning the Australopithecus, the primate who was the precursor of man.

Teilhard was more than a scientist. He was a philosopher who, on the basis of scientific observations, opened up new avenues of thought on evolution and the destiny of the human race, which he described with the knowledge of the expert and the inspiration of the poet. But Teilhard was also a Jesuit priest and as such likely to clash with his superiors in his scientific explanation of the origin and development of man. He insisted that his views only concerned the scientific phenomenon of man and were therefore outside the field of metaphysics, though entirely compatible with religious interpretation. Although Jesuits are granted a relative freedom in their non-religious occupations, Teilhard's outspoken theses encountered opposition in the Catholic hierarchy. He was given assignments which amounted to a banishment from France, where he was only permitted to spend his vacations. He was also dissuaded from accepting a chair at the Collège de France and from having his books published during his lifetime.

Teilhard accepted all these limitations of his freedom with good grace and discipline characteristic of the members of the Society of Jesus, though he must have suffered a terrible disillusionment. Without recanting a word of his scientific conclusions, he tried to reach a synthesis between his scientific convictions and his religious faith. By the use of poetic transfiguration he blended his theses into an inspiring vision. Only at the end of his argumentation does he attempt a metamorphosis of scientific thought into Christian imagery that cannot stand the test of objective criticism. This, however, in no way distracts from the cogency and persuasiveness of his scientific reasoning.

Teilhard wrote seven books, all published posthumously, * of which two were translated into English. In these books Teilhard proceeds from the assumption that man is a

* "Le Phénomène Humain", "Le Milieu Divin", "La Vision du Passé", "L'Apparition de l'Homme", "L'Avenir de l'Homme", "L'Energie Humaine" and "L'Activation de l'Energie".

phenomenon which can be observed both as an individual and in conjunction with mankind as a species. On this basis he develops a number of scientific theories and hypotheses which are summarized below. Divested of their inspiring and often poetic wording they offer a poor substitute for the original, which should give the reader an added incentive to study Teilhard's books themselves. For our purpose, namely to ascertain the trend of modern science and its possible repercussions on contemporary politics, the essence rather than the modalities of Teilhard's thinking is decisive.

The Stuff the Universe is Made of

According to Teilhard, evolution is a process of continual transformation of the simplest kind of matter into more and more complicated forms. Matter progresses from elementary corpuscles, positive and negative protons, neutrons, electrons, etc. to simple substances ranging all the way from hydrogen to uranium, and hence to the immense variety of composite bodies in which molecular masses accumulate. Once these have reached a critical limit, life appears. During this entire development there is not a single element which is not composed of a nucleus and electrons. This reveals the fundamental law that in the entire universe all bodies are derived from an initial corpuscular type. Science definitely established that from the most distant beginnings the stuff of which the universe is made reveals itself in a state of continued creation. At first there was a tendency toward granulation which produced the atom and then, starting from the molecules, a tendency towards increasing complication and perfection.

Energy

That is not all. Matter is not made by adding atoms or placing them side by side. Something more is needed, something that binds them together and brings forth their inner cohesion. A mysterious force pervading the entire universe and all forms of life, which science calls energy and which makes the universe one and indivisible. It is this cosmic energy, linking the infinitely small and the immensely distant, from which all originates and into which all falls back, the

89

immutable, impersonal force which directs evolution. It transforms corpuscles into more and more complicated entities. In the course of these endless transformations no measurable energy ever appears. And yet nothing new can be constructed without an equivalent loss of energy elsewhere. Or so, at least, do the laws of thermo-dynamics teach. To classical scientists the universe is still a closed quantum in which no progression is possible except by exchange of some of the originally available energy. The problem is further complicated by the fact that during every physico-chemical transformation a fraction of energy is lost in the form of heat. Consequently the more actively the universe's energetic quantum functions, the more it uses itself up. It follows that the material universe is unable to pursue indefinitely its course. Its development is limited. It belongs to the realities that are born, mature and die.

If Teilhard is prepared to accept an end to the material universe, this does not, however, imply that he believes in an end to evolution. With the disappearance of matter he assumes that evolution will continue as a psychic phenomenon. Otherwise evolution would defeat its own purpose, something irreconcilable with its achievements today. As to the problem of an otherwise unaccountable universal attrition and disintegration called entropy, Teilhard offers a way out by introducing the concept of psychic energy. It hints at the fact that the second law of thermo-dynamics with its loss of energy might no longer apply to the evolutionary process.

Teilhard posits the existence of two kinds of cosmic forces, centripetal and centrifugal, which create a rhythm that appears everywhere in nature. He bases their existence on his observation of the two main tendencies of evolution, which are the coherence of everything in the universe, and their constant "complexification", a word he coined to describe the way in which everything in the universe becomes increasingly complicated and refined. He ascribes the cohesive forces to centrifugal, and the complexifying ones to centripetal energy.

Centrifugal energy radiating from the surface of particles causes them to attract other particles of the same order and coalesce with them into larger units. In this way combinations of atoms grow into molecules, these into super-molecules ultimately to attain the size of cells, which form the basic units of living organisms of which man is the final outcome to date. Centripetal energy is the force with an inward drive towards the core bringing it into a state of ever greater perfection. Centrifugal energy, by creating larger units and giving them greater mass, activates and strengthens centripetal energy in them. These, with their now more refined cores, in turn radiate stronger centrifugal energy. And so the alternation continues, creating ever larger units with ever more complicated cores until the advent of life.

Teilhard tries to convey with the help of an image how the centrifugal and centripetal energies operate. He attributes to every entity, from the smallest particle to man, a "without" and a "within". Centrifugal energy holds together the "without" of these entities and centripetal energy continuously refines the "within". To this day chemists only deal with the "without" of chemical compounds, and biologists do the same with living cells. This continues with invertebrates and even with vertebrates. Only in man can there no longer be any doubt that the "without" is matched by a "within". Reasoning backwards, Teilhard postulates that this "within" must somehow be present in every particle, because in a universe in which all elements are intrinsically linked, any transformation from a simpler to a more complex form would be unthinkable unless the preceding form contained potentially all the properties of the succeeding. Teilhard specifically warns not to confuse the image of the "within" and "without" with such unscientific distinctions as body and soul. In fact, the image rather conveys that of a gradual metamorphosis of matter into mind and helps to clarify the nature of evolution.

Evolution

To him evolution is an uninterrupted process. In a universe in which nothing is static and nothing stands apart, evolution moves like a stream in which every particle, every element and every creature is caught up and linked together in unbreakable solidarity. Not a single molecule could be removed, ex hypothesis, without the entire structure of the universe collapsing. Evolution is a phenomenon that can be observed as any other. It is a continuous genesis in which the most primitive units change into ever more complicated forms which, to date, have culminated in man.

Evolution is no smoothly running process. It progresses in spurts, sometimes in paroxisms, and looking back on the billions of years of its duration, a few critical points of transformation can be retained on its mounting curve which do not repeat themselves. One of these is the advent of life, a later one the advent of conscious thought. The change from prehominid (when man hovered between primate and primitive man) to homo sapiens, i.e. the awakening of thought, is not only a critical point crossed by the individual and the species, it affects life in its totality and consequently the planet itself. Through man the stuff of which the universe is made starts to think.

The tremendous changes that have occurred in the immensity of evolution's past, among which are the genesis of our planet, of life and of conscious thought, permit us to anticipate equally formidable changes in the future. The most powerful imagination cannot hope to foresee their nature, but certain indications can give a clue to a likely direction evolution is to take.

Life

Life is the product of evolution. Born from gaseous masses, our planet solidified and in the process microscopic particles coalesced into atoms and simple molecules. Under the influence of radiation some of these were transformed into nitrogen compounds called amino acids.* They were dissolved in a sort of "soup" formed by primeval oceans. Radiations falling on this soup produced new reactions leading to the formation of larger organic molecules, some of which, in the course of millions of years, developed the power of self-reproduction.

Life began with the cell. Transition from ultra-microscopic, inanimated particles to microscopic living cells happened imperceptibly. The cell's symmetrical structure, its simplicity, tiny dimensions and identity with other cells link it both qualitatively and quantitatively to the molecules that

---

* These assumptions have been confirmed by laboratory experiments carried out by Dr. Kistiowsky of Harvard, who converted gases by radiation and electric discharges into organic molecules.

form the physico-chemical world of matter. Recent discoveries of heavy molecules which bridge the chasm between life-bearing protoplasm and mineral matter support this hypothesis. However, granted that there is a similarity between cells and inanimate particles, this does not alter the fact that living cells show some remarkable peculiarities which distinguish them from matter. As Teilhard explains in a living cell all molecules are asymmetric in the same way, which means that if pierced by a beam of polarized light they all turn the plane of the beam in the same direction and all either gyrate to the right or to the left. Moreover, all living creatures from the simplest bacteria to man contain exactly the same complicated types of vitamins and enzymes among a potentially infinite number of choices. All animals present identical solutions to the problems of perception, nutrition and reproduction. All have vascular and nervous systems, one or the other form of blood, gonads, eyes, and all show the same trend for individuals to associate.

From this observation Teilhard draws the conclusion that the advent of life on earth is a unique and irreversible event. Only once could the chemistry of the earth create the right conditions for producing protoplasm. They are not likely to occur again due to the fact that the appearance of life disturbed and impoverished the chemistry of the earth to such an extent that the phenomenon cannot be duplicated. Teilhard's conclusion from this that life is an irreversible event, as well as his conclusion, mentioned later, that the advent of conscious thought is a unique occurrence, are important arguments for his contention that evolution has a definite purpose with a direct bearing on man's destiny.

When cells reached the stage of reproduction through splitting, the result was a tremendous expansion and diversification. A-sexual reproduction was followed by sexual mechanism and this prodigious innovation helped to cover the earth with a varied and all-enveloping film of life, a kind of diffused super-organism in which all living particles interact and influence each other. Already in the cell stage life revealed the evolutionary solidarity which, among higher organisms, grew into a network of organic ties which Teilhard calls the "biosphere".

Under the impact of centrifugal energy, living cells agglomerated. The process led from aggregates of bacteria to cell colonies in plants, and from there to higher forms of association culminating in the society of man. Association represents a universal and constant mechanism for the expansion of life and, as such, plays a prominent part in evolution.

As Teilhard sees it, life operates with profusion, inventiveness and indifference. Also with waste and harshness. All that counts is the struggle for life, not for individual existence. This multiplies the chances of survival of the fittest, of natural selection and thus of advance. In nature's blind groping the individual entity has become a mere link. Through association it extends into space, through heredity into time. Life is more important than a life. And so we observe the eternal interaction between centrifugal energy that creates the multiple out of the single, forcing the world towards a state of global unity, and the centripetal energy creating the single out of the multiple. This interaction which pervades the entire course of evolution is, in our time, reflected in the struggle between individualism and the totalisation of mankind.

Another of Teilhard's views on the nature of life has an indirect bearing on the problems with which this book deals. According to him life advances by spurts caused by shocks. Just as man needs an external shock to shake him loose from his natural inertia, habits and environment, so does evolution need violent reactions between material and psychic currents to organize its creative efforts. These shocks, however, would not be able to overcome the fundamental inertia of matter if there were no inner urge in life, the same urge that causes favorable mutations to maintain themselves and unfavorable ones to disappear. This assumption does not solve the mystery of life, but it permits us to envisage an unbroken process of evolution without supernatural intervention. Changes observed in evolution are no new and independent creations, they are transformations.

Man and the Advent of Conscious Thought

Since the beginning of history and until a recent past, man considered himself as the center of the universe. Less than two generations ago science began to reveal the immensity of the universe, and archaeological discoveries to prove that man is the product of an infinitely slow process of development ranging from invertebrates, some 600 million years ago; to vertebrates, 480 million years; and mammals, 190 million years, among whom the primates originated 75 million years ago as man's predecessors.

When a million or more years ago the first intermediate form between primate and man picked up a stick or a sharp stone to serve as weapon or instrument, spontaneous thought was born. When hundreds of thousands of years later new generations no longer waited to find such stones but decided to shape them themselves, conscious thought and with it homo sapiens made his appearance. It took nature numerous experiments to produce contemporary man. From such border types as the Olduvai man, 1,700,000 years ago, and the Australopithecus Africanus, 600,000 years ago, to the Peking and Java man, 500,000 years ago, the first to have known fire, the giant men who lived some 300,000 years ago on different continents, the more recent Neanderthal man of 70,000 years ago, who probably was a side-branch, there finally emerged some 30 to 40,000 years ago the Cro-Magnon and Aurignac men, who, in appearance, artistic capabilities and potential ability for rational thought, stand very near to present man.

Their cave paintings in the South of France and in Spain bear witness of an unsurpassed artistic talent, sense of observation, imagination and creative urge. Their animistic rites show understanding for the intangible. Since no biological changes of any importance occurred between the Cro-Magnon and Aurignac men and present man, and the former were endowed with sensibility, conscience, courage and reflection, the question arises how to explain the tremendous change that took place in the outward appearance of the world. A change as evidenced by the cities, industrial installations, roads, bridges, railways, power lines that cover the earth, ships that cross the oceans, and planes that fly overhead. To have been able to change his environment to such a degree in a comparatively short span of time, man himself must have considerably changed. And as the change did not occur in his body, it must have happened in his mind. As past changes of the brain capacity in the animal world were extremely slow, as slow as their physical mutations, the conclusion to be reached is that a new system of heredity has begun to operate in man besides the old genetic system. In the millions of years since the advent of life, mutations occurred so slowly as to be imperceptible in the gradual alteration of the physical aspects of the species. With the advent of man evolution got a new rhythm. Not during the first million years when man groped his way from pre-hominid to homo sapiens, but during the past millennia, since man reached a certain stage of conscious thought. Then evolution operated no longer on his body but on his mind. A new non-genetic system of heredity is occasioning changes in man's mind, brought about by knowledge, skills and ideas transmitted from one generation to another. A system that is infinitely faster than genetic mutations and which, according to Teilhard, seems to contradict the hitherto irrefutable axiom that acquired characteristics cannot be inherited.

There is another point to be noted. When thinking of the evolution of man, we see in our mind's eye a creature half primate, half man, changing into Peking man and via a number of other transformations to homo sapiens. But we give little attention to the tribe, race, nation and lately to the more and more compressed influence which mankind has on the individual's evolution. Notwithstanding all his inventiveness and the help of machines he created, man would have been unable to give the world its present aspect without close cooperation with other men. This cooperation is increased by a convergence of the human race which is becoming more and more pronounced.

The Convergence of Mankind

As Teilhard describes it the convergence of mankind is a comparatively recent development, having set in some twenty thousand years ago. In its remote past, during the pre-sapiens and para-sapiens phase, the human zoological group showed distinct traces of divergent ramification common to all pre-human phyla. As a further symptom of its immaturity, it proved incapable of reaching out beyond the limits of the territory where it was born. However, from the High Paleolithic on, i.e. the time of the Cro-Magnon and Aurignac man, biological differentiation disappeared and the various races, white, black, yellow and brown, did not spread into opposite directions, increasing the difference between them, but converged. The main hearth of hominization* spread from subtropical Africa to the Mediterranean Zones and from there all over the globe via Northern Europe, and via Siberia to the two Americas. It was then that through inter-penetration and interbreeding differences gradually levelled off and the human species began to fuse into a single entity.

Teilhard calls the present convergence of mankind, which manifests itself in the growing solidarity of the human race and the interdependence of all individuals, a phenomenon of "socialization", i.e. the growth of heterogeneous parts into a single entity. Far from being an accidental phenomenon, this close association of mankind represents on the curve of evolution a development of the same order and magnitude as the advent of life and of conscious thought. We may not be able to realize its impetus—for it is always difficult to discern the great lines of evolution in the midst of one's daily life—but there is no mistaking the fact that in our highly complicated society each individual has to such a degree become dependent on others that no living being could long survive if left to his own devices. No man can live by his own thoughts alone, his consciousness is a medium that can only vibrate through its contact with other such media. As Claude Cuénot remarks in a commentary on Teilhard, man-kind possesses a single physics, a single chemistry, a single oil and steel industry, and a single organized research for finding the answers to a single series of problems. In this connection Teilhard himself points out that the present progress of technology does not present a series of local achievements but a geotechnology spreading all over the globe.

Imperceptibly the center of gravity shifts from the in-dividual to the collectivity. The process is accelerated by the population explosion. To use a Newtonian formula: it seems as if the inborn enmity between people diminishes by the square of the distance between them. There is no doubt that over and above national and racial barriers and divergent ideologies, mankind is achieving an increasing cohesion. This happens under a constantly growing pressure comparable to the force which holds the planets together in a single system. The resultant is mankind as a synthesis which is more than

---

* Hominization = the progressive change from animal to conscious human life.

the sum of its individuals, just as man is more than the sum of the particles of which he is composed. Mankind's "totalisation" reveals itself in the fact that everywhere the masses become conscious of themselves. This does not cause them to rise in order to overthrow an existing order, or to hasten the cycle of the renewal of classes. Their consciousness is of a different order. It rather resembles the groundswell of an inexorable movement towards world interdependence and solidarity.

The Sphere of Inter-Thinking

Man's primordial urge to concentrate on himself has always been counterbalanced by his relationship to other men. With the sharpening of his mental capacities, the thoughtwaves emanating from him grew stronger. His thoughts flowed out to others, met theirs and slowly a web of thought was spun around the world. Teilhard calls this the "noosphere" or sphere of inter-thinking, an organism which shows remarkable similarities with Haskin's "cultural society". It is with the help of this noosphere that man was able to launch the collective effort needed for changing the face of the earth to what it is today.

At first the noosphere was only loosely knit, but it already heralded the solid thinking envelope which encloses mankind today with a network of communications that evokes the image of a nervous system. As Teilhard describes it, if a man from Mars armed with a super-spectroscope observed the earth, he would see the noosphere lit up by the crackling of millions of criss-crossing thought waves sparking one another. The formation of the inter-thinking organism is facilitated by the curvature of the earth which forces thought waves to converge into a sphere. Thus they are prevented from losing themselves in the universe and are compressed into a think layer around the earth.

With the formation of the inter-thinking organism, evolution entered into a new phase. The totalisation of the human race is no longer—as in the case of animals—a biological process, but has become a process of social organization directed by man's mind. With the advent of homo sapiens all evolutionary changes, both of the individual and of the race, are concentrated in the mind.* The sudden and irresistible tide of cerebration of the past few hundred years brought a change of planetary magnitude to the earth.

Mutations, no longer retarded by infinitely slow biological processes, occur in the mind with unprecedented speed. Man is forever driven to think faster. This heightens man's originality and inventiveness, helps him to throw off the shackles of conventional thought and widens his mental horizon. Man thus obtains a better insight into causality and probability, learns to rely on his own judgment, sharpens his foresight and accelerates his powers of rationalization.

The inter-thinking organism or, to use Julian Huxley's expression, the "single pool of common thought", is greatly helped by modern means of communication that put an end to parochial inhibitions. The written, spoken and televised word breaks down thought-tight compartments. World trade, cultural exchanges, scientific cooperation and numerous other exchanges force new impressions on people everywhere and make them think, discuss and continuously make up and remake up their own minds. As Teilhard describes it, the exchange of millions of thoughts increases the psychic tension and inner coalescence of the noosphere. The psychic temperature rises and with it the mental activity of mankind. This, in turn, stimulates the individual's thinking processes which further promotes the growth of the inter-thinking organism. Thus a self-perpetuating interaction is generated.

In the noosphere lies the genesis of a totally new element in the course of evolution, which Huxley calls the "rudiments of a head". A somewhat similar idea occurred to J.B.S. Haldane as quoted by Teilhard. In his "Essay on Science and Ethics" Haldane writes: "Now, if the cooperation of some thousands of millions of cells in our brain can produce our consciousness, the idea becomes vastly more plausible that the cooperation of humanity, or some sections of it, may determine what (the French philosopher Auguste) Comte calls a Great Being". This super-brain's task would be to gradually emancipate an as yet incipient mankind from the hold of matter and carry it forward into the realm of the spirit. In a grandiose flight of phantasy, Teilhard visualizes

---

* This is called anthropogenesis, indicating that in man biological evolution gives way to cultural evolution.

a noosphere leaving behind its material womb in order to rise into the world of the spirit, establish psychic ties with other spheres of consciousness across the universe and form an ultimate center of consciousness. It is there that the psychic energies accumulated in the noosphere will escape when life ceases on this planet. And it is there that the irreversible process of evolution will continue after the human phenomenon has come to an end, provided that meanwhile mankind avoids a suicidal cataclysm or that the earth is spared a planetary collision. But such occurrences are unlikely, because man's emergence is so fantastic and his evolution such an improbable event that it would make no sense for the experiment not to reach its ultimate fulfilment. *

To return to earth and in order not to anticipate events that may be as far off in the future as the advent of life was in the past (though evolutionary transformations in the sphere of the mind will undoubtedly be faster than in the sphere of matter), an impartial observer may well ask whether the pressure exercised by the noosphere may not lead to conformism of thought and thus deeply affect the human race as Haskins and other biologists fear. The swarming of mankind all over the globe and the ensuing population explosion were obviously necessary for the proper functioning of the noosphere, but will they not ultimately lead to an uncontrollable catastrophe that spells the end of the human race and of nature's effort to give a psychic turn to the human experiment?

Teilhard is aware of the problem and mentions several of the possible dangers resulting from the geometric progression of the population coupled to the not less rapid increase of the individual's "volume", i.e. his radius of action on the surface of the globe. These dangers are: Rapid exhaustion of the earth's food and raw material resources;
Levelling off and disappearance of the differences which hitherto produced the rich varieties in man's efforts, under a neutral and homogeneous cultural layer;

* As the biological cycles of animal life which preceded that of man averaged 80 million years and as the development of conscious thought is in its very beginning, we can expect an immense duration before the end of human evolution is reached.

100

Mechanisation of individual values and thoughts; and Breaking up of national identities with corresponding degradation and de-humanisation of mankind.

But Teilhard does not share these dark forebodings because he believes that the same forces which caused mankind to converge will ere long cause it to contract. Mankind is just now embarking upon the delicate adjustment from dilation to contraction, which is likely to be a painful process. Having been able to survive the preceding stages of reflection and co-reflection, there is no reason why the present stage of totalisation which the human race is entering is not also likely to produce a step forward. Far from showing any indication of decay, mankind gives the impression of having reached the plenitude of psychic genesis and of being in the act of creating something totally new in the way of evolution.

About the danger that the sphere of inter-thinking will lead to conformism in thought or create a collective conscience which levels off the demands of man's individual conscience as well as his originality and creativity to become to all practical intents and purposes identical to the goal which Communism pursues, Teilhard is not alarmed. Menacing as the trend towards conformism looks for our individual liberties, ultimate integration of mankind becomes impossible from the moment that we realize that man's spiritual evolution cannot be achieved without resort to his deepest individual resources and originality. The same forces that operate towards totalisation of the human race, constantly increase the individual's cerebration pushing him towards ever larger rationalization, understanding and spirituality. The movement towards unification of mankind in the direction of an inter-thinking organism is compensated by another movement towards ever greater complexification of the individual in the direction of what Teilhard calls "personalization".

Man's Personalization

By "personalization" Teilhard understands the purposeful endeavour of the individual to find his inner core, to "know himself" and by intensifying his thinking capacity to gain a growing insight into the forces of nature and the universe as they reflect themselves in his own mind. To achieve this, man has to keep intact his independence and originality of thought. This, in turn, provides him with a measure of fore-sight and free decision permitting him to influence the direction of his life.* In this way the blind evolutionary groping which nature conducts through biological mutations can, in the human being, be replaced and hastened by a process of thought mutations.

The advance in man's thinking, though still haphazard and unbalanced, has shown itself in discoveries and inventions in a number of fields. These are mostly connected with special-ized and technical matters, but there is also an overall field in which man's thinking has taken a new flight. For the first time he is becoming aware of the space-time continuum, i.e. he is learning to think in a new dimension. There is also, still in its infancy, the tendency to replace mysticism, which brought man hope but also suffering and frustration, by rational approaches. Man is becoming increasingly aware that science is the only instrument to express his spiritual destiny in rational terms.

Man's thinking, moreover, helps him to overcome his egotism. By self-realization man rises above individualism to attain personality. He becomes less self-centered, less swayed by instincts and superstitions. He no longer keeps his innermost thoughts and perceptions to himself, but learns to share his ego with others. In this way man's personalization promotes the unification of mankind which, in its deepest sense, can only spring from a meeting of the inner core of all individuals. From it alone can emanate the love which is able to replace man's instinctive hostility to other men and make him feel one with them. On the other hand, there can be no doubt that if the collectivity were ultimately to absorb such personalized individual, it would destroy this love. It follows that man's evolution demands both the personalization of the individual and the unification of mankind.

---

* Some 150 years ago the French philosopher Fabre d'Olivet, a contemporary of Napoleon, writing about the forces that govern the universe, distinguished between fate, providence and man's will. Though his thoughts were based on intuition and not on scientific observation, he already recognized in man's will the mitigating factor in an otherwise rigid determinism.

102

Our individualistic instincts still rebel against the trend towards totalisation, but this is likely to change with a better understanding of the mechanism of evolution. Having experienced how the steady refinement of the individual's mind generates ever greater psychic forces, we should also realise that man, too, must follow the evolutionary law which bundles smaller entities into larger ones. Whether we like it or not, no power on earth can help us to escape mankind's totalisation, because in this evolution the power of the universe reveals itself. What we seem to forget is that the rebundling of individuals into an organism, comprising the totality of mankind, is bound to release further psychic energies which, in turn, will raise the individual to a higher level. Because cosmic forces operate simultaneously, it is unthinkable that this "personalization" of the individual does not take place "pari-passu" with the "totalisation" of mankind, or that the development of the noosphere would be possible without a further perfectioning of the individual's core.

For the time being, we cannot get away from the impression that totalisation in whatever form is being forced upon mankind. Teilhard thinks that only from the time that man understands that every human being is being solidary with a single convergent "all", can there be question of a free totalisation and can coercion be replaced by voluntary cooperation in mutual sympathy. Today all we see around us are violently clashing ideas, ideologies and passions.

Yet another process is going on, according to Teilhard, partly hidden but partly visible to those able to take a little distance from what happens around them. During the past war it looked as if parts of the world were definitely going to be torn asunder. And what happened? Only a few years after the war the Pacific area, great parts of which had remained outside the pale of modern civilization, was entirely drawn into the industrial orbit. Mechanization reached the most remote corners of the world. Nations that went to war to disengage themselves found that each successive war knit them more inextricably together. The more they tried to repel each other, the deeper their interpenetration became. Vast armies followed by millions of refugees permeated the populations of other nations, planting new ideas everywhere. Infinitely diversified ways of living fused into a similar pattern. All over the world nations are caught in a process of integration advancing in jerks. Though the present ideological fight seems to split the world into two irreconcilable camps that may ultimately annihilate one another, a countermovement is developing rooted in a growing sense of solidarity and interdependence among the masses. This may help to break up the rigidity of the ideological conflict and lead to the abandonment of apparently unshakable positions whereby the forces of repulsion and attraction are held in suspence. Mankind will possibly have to go through a long period of strife and uncertainty before it is ready to unite voluntarily. One thing is certain, the compass points towards ever closer unification. In spite of everything, man's personalization and mankind's totalisation seem to proceed. What our world is facing is a reorientation of the phenomenon of man into new social and spiritual orbits.

We do not know how this is going to happen. We can only suppose that the polarity between personalized man and a humanity increasingly conscious of its biological and psychic unity will generate violent tensions. As always in nature, these tensions occasion spasmodic advances as well as crises, one of which has landed us in our present ideological strife.

In an effort to assess the significance of mankind's evolution as thus presented by Teilhard, the eons of time stretching back into the past that were needed to produce man have to be projected into the future if we ever hope to approximate the possibilities which man's forward march offers. Considering the tremendous changes that took place in man's thinking and environment during the past thousands and even hundreds of years, we can conclude that what is still in store for him must be infinitely more sweeping and totally beyond present comprehension. Just as atoms had already hidden within them the potentialities of life, man is likely to carry within himself the seeds of a spiritual energy that will permit him to attain his ultimate liberation from matter and mankind to attain immortality.

Chapter X

COMMENTS ON AND RESPONSE TO
THE MODERN THEORY OF EVOLUTION

In our short summary of the concepts of the new science of
evolution, we attempted to outline some general principles
which have a direct bearing on our political problem and to
which we will return in Chapter XIII. It would be premature
to believe that people are already able to draw political
conclusions from the theory of evolution. But, especially in
Europe, the response to it has been distinctively favorable.

Though there is a certain reserve in scientific circles, as
is usually the case with bold and new ideas and hypotheses, in
continental Western Europe, Teilhard's undoubtedly difficult
books are being sold by the thousands, while a large number
of Teilhard societies and debating centers have been organized.* And, what is more telling, a number of his conclusions
and hypotheses are being confirmed in other fields of science.

Cosmic Energy

Meticulous observations by modern biologists brought to light
the fact that each mature individual possesses some hundred
trillion cells, each of which contains forty-eight chromosomes
through which hereditary properties are transmitted. Each
chromosome contains a thousand genes that hold what may
be called a shorthand formula of all different properties of
man from the color of his eyes to the rhythm of his heartbeat. And each gene, in turn, is made up of about a million
atoms. This led to the hypothesis that man's hereditary
characteristics are determined by the distribution of
these atoms within the structure of the genes. If we ponder
the question of by what force this distribution is produced, it

* The Ford Foundation gave a grant of $ 25,000 in order to
convene an international conference in the U.S. for study and
discussion of Teilhard's ideas.

looks as if biology stumbled upon a clue for the operation of cosmic energy on man as postulated by the theory of evolution.

Cosmology

In Chapter VI, page 62, we remarked that the impossibility of an all-embracing cosmic observation forces scientists to fall back on philosophical instead of factual assumptions on which to build an hypothesis. This is what the authors of the Steady State theory did when they postulated a universe without beginning or end, in eternal evolution, and comprising an unending series of generations of galaxies. If one of these were to disintegrate, the result would not be total annihilation as under the Explosion theory, nor total disappearance when one cycle passes into another as under the Expansion-Contraction theory. The Steady State theory postulates the coexistence of different generations of galaxies as well as the possibility that accumulated knowledge and experience gained in one galaxy can be passed on to another during their unending succession. This ties in with the theory of evolution and offers a remarkable analogy with the role played by mankind's pool of common thinking in transmitting experience and knowledge, and with the hypothesis of this pool's potential ties with other similar centers of consciousness in the universe.

Heredity

Recent hypotheses of contemporary biologists on heredity offer another confirmation of one of Teilhard's conclusions. We saw on page 96 of the preceding chapter that Teilhard postulates that with man a new kind of non-genetic heredity appeared. An heredity through which experience and knowledge are transmitted from one generation to the other, and which contradicts the hitherto generally accepted rule that acquired characters cannot be inherited. Most biologists still cling to this axiom, but recently some of them arrived at a conclusion similar to that of Teilhard. In his book "The Future of Man", the well-known biologist P. B. Medawar explains that "the environment cannot imprint genetical information upon us, but it can and does imprint non-genetical information which we can and do pass on. Acquired characteristics are indeed inherited". No wonder that biologists are changing their minds. They are faced with the obvious fact of present-day man's growing ability to assimilate knowledge of the past. Everywhere the phenomenon can be observed that each succeeding generation of children learns more easily and is more precocious than the preceding one. It is evident that children inherit the ability of assimilating knowledge. The question is how. If not through genes, it may be conjectured that it happens under the pressure of the layer of thought-waves that envelop the world and act as a generator. Today of the fourteen billion cells which the human brain contains, scientists assume that over 90 per cent are still unused. Under the impact of the noosphere more and more of these braincells or neurones are put into operation, adding new circuits to the computing machinery of the mind. It is this capacity which is being inherited by man's offspring and which makes every new generation more receptive to learning and to storing knowledge.

Noosphere

We already mentioned that Auguste Comte and Caryl Haskins anticipated the noosphere or inter-thinking organism, the former with his "Great Being", the latter with his "cultural society", and that no less an authority than Julian Huxley adopted the concept of thought-waves surrounding the earth and called them "mankind's rudimentary head". Today more scientists are inclined to agree that this layer of thought-waves affects the depth and width of thinking over the entire globe. They ascribe to the common rhythm of thinking a unifying effect which, notwithstanding all existing divergencies, gives an overall direction to the thoughts of all. It determines the pace of science's advance, and explains the fact that discoveries and inventions are made simultaneously and independently in various places on earth. It also helps to form a world opinion* and to develop a world conscience that pro-

---

* To Political Scientists such a way of thinking is still un-familiar. In an article "Is World Public Opinion a Myth?" Professor Hans Morgenthau writes that "humanity is not con-stituted as one great society pursuing common aims, but as a multitude of national societies, reflecting the most diverse conditions, interests and aspirations". No one denies the

vokes a greater similarity of reactions everywhere. Finally it forms, in our present stage of development, an only vaguely perceived collective brain which spans the world, stimulates receptivity, speeds up the pace of change and enables mankind to recognize and partially guide the direction of its evolution.

Criticism of the Modern Theory of Evolution

Orthodoxy

Direct opposition to the modern theory of evolution comes from those who deny that life can spring from "dead" matter and that man endowed with a soul* can descend from animals that have none. According to them both life and soul require a special act of divine creation. This is a matter of metaphysics which lies beyond the scope of this study, but it is certainly not paying less reverence to God to consider evolution a continuous act of the Creator than to ascribe it to a series of special divine interventions. In the field of science the miraculous and the supernatural cannot be accepted as explanations of an observed phenomenon. Science did observe that life came on earth after the advent of matter and that life exemplifies the everywhere apparent phenomenon that the more complicated follows upon the less complex in the process of evolution. Science concluded that the advent of

existence of different societies, the point being that one then also must admit that each society consists in turn of conflicting interest groups, parties, etc. By following Morgenthau's approach this leads to a tangle of contradictory local opinions. Just as nations gained an identity of their own by creating a predominant national public opinion, the world community is on its way to arriving at a world public opinion indicative of its tendency towards oneness. Instead of denying the rise of such world opinion, it is in the interest of mankind to activate it by all possible means. And the first of these is to recognize its existence. No more than a national public opinion prevents diversity of opinions within the nation, will a world opinion prevent global diversity.

* According to H. G. Wells, Julian Huxley and G. P. Wells in "The Science of Life" the concept soul has never been scientifically established.

life constitutes the elusive moment that matter crossed the threshold from molecule to cell, a moment that could only occur once when conditions on earth were exactly right for it. This does not mean that similar conditions could not be created artificially. Scientists believe that it is only a matter of time before life can be created in a laboratory in the same way as when chemical compounds and molecules were exposed to certain radiations in far-away ages. This view is neither materialistic nor atheistic. To visualize the advent of life and later the coming of conscious thought as the budding, after a long period of perfecting and refinement, of attributes potentially dormant in every cosmic particle, surpasses in spiritual depth a too literal interpretation of the Scriptures. At the same time it offers a scientific hypothesis which covers the observed phenomena without recourse to supernatural intervention. For the first time the myth of supernatural (but not of divine) creation has been scientifically disproved, and the scientific hypothesis which replaces it is more inspiring, and miraculous, than the myth itself.

Man's Uniqueness

Another aspect of the new theory of evolution requires clarification. Teilhard considers the advent of life and of conscious thought as unique events. No exception can be taken to this statement, if it means that they can only occur once in the course of evolution. But what can only happen once in the evolution on our planet is not necessarily unique. Modern scientists reason that if only one in every three million stars possesses conditions similar to those on earth—which looks like a certainty according to the laws of probability—there will be among the trillions of stars millions on which evolution will reach, has reached or is surpassing the present stage of man's development. * If the evolutionary experiment is

---

* Scientists convinced of the existence of life on other stars try to make radio contact with them through radio telescopes as the one in Puerto Rico which can pick up signals from stars 12 billion light years away. In view of stages of evolution surpassing ours and their efforts to reach other stars, they hope to intercept some kind of coded message such as Planck's constant, i.e. the fixed value whereby the frequency of a quantum of radiation must be multiplied to determine its energy.

not restricted to our planet but conducted on thousands or even millions of stars, its success is no longer dependent on the human race, but may find its ultimate development somewhere else. We must conclude that man may not be a unique phenomenon, even though one that can only occur once in the course of an evolution which itself, however, is likely to take place on a number of stars.

Once again man seems to have been wronged. Having already found out that he is not the center of the universe, his uniqueness as evolutionary phenomenon is now equally questioned. But the fact that evolution may take place on different stars does not relieve him from his responsibility. Quite to the contrary, it increases it. For if the evolutionary experiment is conducted on various stars, it no longer would be a logical absurdity for evolution to abort on earth, and it would become more and more dependent upon man himself whether his destiny will soar ever higher or end in a disaster for which he is to be blamed.

It may not be too bold a suggestion that experiments in evolution on other stars encountered crises such as the one through which mankind now passes. Nor is it improbable that some evolutions have been able to overcome these crises while others succumbed to them. Teilhard's contention that man's evolution on earth must succeed because it otherwise would be senseless, is therefore too parochial. However, this takes nothing away from the reassurance which mankind can derive from his grandiose vision on evolution. It frees man from the feeling of frustration that all his toil and suffering are in vain in a life in which there is neither rhyme nor reason. It gives a goal to life, and to the human race a sense of continuity. True, mankind can destroy on this planet all which evolution achieved in billions of years. But then man is the culprit and not a blind fate over which he has no say.

Finally, there is the question whether the similarity of evolution on earth, from cell to animal, reflects a universal tendency of evolution or a local, terrestrial, variety. According to J. Robert Oppenheimer, the universe contains particles unknown on earth. Although fossilized cells found in meteors a billion years old show traces of nucleid acid, they differ from cells on earth by possessing no nuclei. This suggests the possibility that life elsewhere need not resemble life on earth.

110

This excursion into cosmology was not to add a touch of the sensational to our narrative, but to underline the fact that human problems must be envisaged in their widest possible perspective, something which cannot be achieved without close cooperation of the best brains all over the world. It also shows how futile the present division of the world looks and how the ideological struggle that loomed so high in our preoccupations can dwindle in comparison with the basic issues mankind is up against.

Future Evolution

A final comment concerns Teilhard's thoughts on the future of evolution. We already mentioned his vision that from the meeting of millions of conscious minds on earth, a super-mind emerges which, in an infinite future, is to form the ultimate center of consciousness. It is in this center of consciousness, which he equates with Christ, that Teilhard finds his synthesis between science and religion.

This vision impinges too much on the field of metaphysics to lend itself to a scientific analysis, though it may be re-marked in passing that Teilhard's particular synthesis may well have been prompted by a desire to give greater elevation to current Christian symbolism. In many a Christian rite, symbolism has been replaced by dogmatism and Teilhard may have felt that this distortion of symbolism involves a danger of changing religion into superstition. In his final vision on evolution, Christ is no longer tied to any form of matter or to this planet, and has become the symbol of evolution's highest achievement.

Teilhard's philosophy behind this apotheosis of evolution is not new. Others have expressed the view that, pursued to its logical end, evolution which created life out of matter and endowed it with conscious thought, must lead to a gradual detachment and liberation from matter, and to the emanci-pation of man's spirit from the physical hold of this planet. The Greek poet Nikos Kazantzakis, author of "The Odyssey, A Modern Sequel", visualized this when he wrote about the transmutation of matter into spirit as man's highest endeavor and used the moving words: "It is the endangered spirit in each man that is crying out for liberation".

111

Contemporary science, too, offers its tentative contribution to man's liberation from this planet by helping him to overcome the earth's gravitational force and break away into space. This also is a feat of spirit over matter and, at the same time, the realization of man's most daring dream.

Back to Earth

Having so far followed the theory of evolution and especially the vision of man's future, the reader may wonder how this image can be reconciled with his daily observations, which show the hold which man's primitive instincts continue to have over him. Man's present preoccupations do not seem to have substantially changed from prehistoric times. Is there a reason to suppose that man's instincts will not continue to prevail over his spiritual orientation and that Teilhard's "personalization" is not a utopia? The answer is that man only stands at the very beginning of his evolution, and that the greatly accelerated improvement of his mind during the most recent past bodes well for the future. Looking ahead, it can be anticipated that the present stage of evolution will be followed by new advances. Man's urge towards self-fulfilment and his awareness of his growing responsibility towards other men, seem to indicate that he is on the right track. For it is between the two poles of self-fulfilment and interdependence that evolution advances and mankind's destiny lies. To quote Julian Huxley: "Man is evolution become conscious of itself".

Chapter XI

CHANGES IN OUR THINKING

Thinking in General

As people become more familiar with the concept of evolution, it begins to influence their thinking and their attitude towards a number of new problems. The theory of evolution's main contribution to modern thinking is the average man's acceptance of change as a normal phenomenon. And indeed evolution is change. During eons of biological mutations changes were so slow as to be imperceptible. Only after man learned to think and mutations mostly occurred in his brain, did the pace of change quicken. In evolution, changes come spasmodically, in spurts. The present breakthrough in science represents such a spurt.

Because in the past these spurts were far apart, the one preceding the present breakthrough having occurred during the Renaissance, man had every reason to think in terms of a static world. What had been good enough for his forefathers was good enough for him. Even a hundred years ago what a man learned at school could carry him through life. Today man has to keep studying to the end of his life to keep up to date. All the time he has to prepare himself for the coming changes. His thinking must of necessity be turned to the future.

After the present breakthrough there will be a period of adaptation. But it is unlikely to last for ten or twelve generations as it did after the Renaissance. It may last for a couple of generations at most, for the more intense the breakthrough the faster man's thinking becomes, and the sooner mutations of his mind will succeed one another. During the present phase, which is still in full swing, man's thoughts are inevitably directed to the responses he has to find to countless new and unexpected challenges. No longer can experiences and formulas of the past be used to solve the problems of tomorrow. In such a period conservatism becomes an anachronism.

Changes in Our Thinking

Obstacles to Man's Thinking

Man's Instincts

There is nothing surprising in man's innate conservatism and inertia. In the first place, man is still bound by primitive instincts and superstitions. He is subject to fear as indicated by his periodical recourse to aggressiveness and lawlessness. Unable sometimes to pursue the fate of man, he sinks back into the jungle where instinct replaces reason. To quieten his conscience he then extolls bestiality and raises it into a fetish. He errs because he has not yet learned to use fully his mental capacities or because he is too lazy to do so. The fears that obsess him are the fears of change, of destitution and of death. The latter is Western man's greatest handicap, which neither Christian religion nor Western civilization has been able to allay. Man's maturing mind hesitates to accept as literal truth the allegory of individual survival in heaven or hell, but neither has he learned the Oriental's acceptance of death as shared by all his forebears in an unbroken rhythm. He, too, might be able to overcome the fear of death by thinking in terms of humanity and its succeeding generations as a whole. Thus seen, he forms a link in an unbreakable chain, and it is this chain, humanity, which gives to each his immortality. But more than fear of change, poverty, and death, unconscious and unreasonable fear is perhaps what plagues man most of all. The kind of fear upon which last century's Wesleyan preacher and today's Communist manipulator thrive. The fear of being abandoned to a life which is a result of blind chance and therefore an absurdity. The fear which today's psychiatrists so often encounter.

This perplexity and despair can be rationalized by explaining to man his place in the scheme of evolution, his relationship to mankind and the latter's potentialities. He can be made secure by imparting to him a sense of continuity in nature, and by making him aware that he serves a definite and indispensable purpose in a great design.

Other Obstacles

Man's thinking is moreover steeped in myths. These can be overcome through knowledge or faith, provided that neither

114

degenerates into dogmatism and is periodically re-thought. For the power to conquer fear and superstition lies in man himself, and neither knowledge nor faith can help him unless they are fully acceptable to his conscience. For no man can have a philosophy which does not surge from his innermost self.

Man has to rely on his mind. This is an arduous task which demands courage and unflinching application. Also humility, since man should beware of the unwarranted assumption —which the old Greeks called "hubris"—that he has reached the present stage of evolution on his own merits. Man is an instrument chosen by nature for its latest experiment in evolution, and only if he learns to live up to it, can he hope to become worthy of the fantastic destiny which nature has in store for him. To achieve this, man must think. But as yet the majority of people refuse to think beyond the immediate range of their daily occupations. It is true that nothing is more difficult than thinking. Descartes once remarked that times were few and far between when he was able to think a purely abstract thought.

There are signs that man is progressing. He begins to understand that many of his aggressive traits result from repressed desires. This gives him a clue for gaining control over himself. Interest in and curiosity about new concepts and wider horizons help him to overcome these desires. He is gradually acquiring a taste for rational thinking, but to this very day some obstacles remain in his way, among which are his inveterate desire to seek refuge in the "good old times" and his emotionalism.

Familiar concepts of the past, and many of its illusions, provide a sense of security. Few people visualize the future with the same intensity as they recall the past. This is natural, for it is difficult to keep up with the pace of changes. Even in the advanced Western democracies most people are inclined to live exclusively in the present. It sometimes seems as if they deliberately shorten their perspective in order to live from day to day. In the United States the man who thinks of the day after tomorrow risks being decried as a visionary. In Europe Sartre's existentialism teaches living from day to day, rejects the notion of God and sees man's existence dependent on blind chance and predicated on his freedom of choice in concrete situations. In a similar way some contemporary Western novelists shy away from conceptual thinking to concentrate on minute details of their characters' daily lives and surroundings, leaving every issue up in the air and by depicting a variety of colors and tones trying to avoid looking into the future.

As to man's emotionalism, it unexpectedly pops up in the midst of an argument or conversation, when he reacts to points that appeal to his emotion, singling these out and ignoring the logical trend. Similarly, people often retain from newspapers, radio or T.V. only what stimulates their emotions. As a result they look for what serves this purpose and thus encourage sensationalism in all our means of communication. Yet it is only through thinking ahead that man was able in the past to master his environment. He evolved in his neuro-cerebral system an instrument permitting him to step, so to say, out of himself and to change from a passive object to an active factor in the shaping of his future. No longer should changes take him by surprise, for they are mostly of his own making. But he is still caught up in a number of thinking habits which prevent him from fully participating in today's general advance.

Our Unscientific Dichotomies

One of our deep-rooted habits is to think in contrasts, in black and white, ignoring all other shades and not realizing that our sharpest distinctions often represent no more than different aspects of one and the same thing. Take, for example, the difference between matter and spirit as postulated by Descartes. Scientifically we know that the solidity of matter is an illusion due to the relative coarseness of our organs of perception which prevents us from observing the happenings in the microcosmos. * The distinction between matter and light or other waves is one of degree, as both consist of the same particles invisible to the human eye, though similar in substance and only assembled in different ways. The spoken word, or man's sound-wave, has been called the boundary between the world of matter and spirit; the thought-wave would have to be classified under the latter concept, and so the difference between matter and spirit is revealed as artificial.

* Cf. Chapter VI, page 62.

116

Other dualisms in our way of thinking are the distinctions we make between body and soul, thought and sentiment, science and religion or, to mention another example, good and bad. Their differences lie in our mind and in our habit of creating dichotomies which do not exist in nature but which we accentuate in order to classify our perceptions, to establish an order of values and thus to facilitate our thinking.

The sharper these distinctions are, the more rigid our attitudes tend to become and the more we lose our independence and elasticity of thought. This tendency has been encouraged throughout man's history by secular and religious authorities alike. They issued laws and moral precepts of what was right and what was wrong. They branded as culprits and sinners all who tried to resist or even discuss their decrees. Sin was what in the realm of mysticism had been revealed as such to the religious authorities and therefore was beyond the individual's ken. Sin became the merciless weapon to cow the peoples everywhere and force them into blind obedience. In our Christian ethics the concept of original sin sapped man's self-confidence, prejudiced his every action and thought, and deprived him of the dignity of independent judgment.

Partly free and aspiring to the stars, partly steeped in "original sin", often pressured to believe what deep in his conscience he rejects, Western man developed a split personality. Acceptance of the moral or political authority of church or state dispensed him from using his own discernment and thinking for himself. Man assumed two sides, partly seeking to conform, partly seeking to find his inner self. His uncertainty was compounded when governments used a double standard of morality, one for themselves called "reason of state", which clashes with our general ethics and in fact is the opposite of morality, and one for the average man.

Under the impact of democracy things improved and freedom of thought and speech were recognized though double morality and its kin, class justice, have not disappeared from the free world's scene. A strong trend towards conformism, which is incompatible with independent thinking, adds to contemporary man's confusion. If man's code of values becomes uncertain, the purpose of his life, the purpose of life itself, escapes him. His joy of living, his creative ability and dynamism suffer. Instead of gaining ascendancy over his environment, he becomes passive, abdicates his right to rational thought, and finally puts up with a number of prejudices and superstitions.

A too rigid distinction between good and bad is equally unrealistic. Every society evidently needs laws, moral codes, and rules of conduct to protect itself. They must provide precise criteria of what is and what is not permitted. Moreover they must be protected against sudden amendments under emotional stress or in times of commotion. But from there it is quite a step to reasoning that without a sharp distinction between good and bad there can be no morality or decency, or that thinking in shades leads to compromise and undermines integrity. On the contrary, the very classification in categories of good and bad presents the individual with a ready-made decision and prevents him from judging according to his conscience. Moreover, there is always some good in the bad and some bad in all good, and it requires intense individual thinking to detect this. The kind of thinking that helps the individual to establish his personal scale of values and to find himself. It also stimulates the necessary periodical revision of laws and moral codes which can only be undertaken upon the urging of individuals or groups who no longer can square existing laws or codes with their changed views. This has happened again and again, proving that there are no absolute criteria of right or wrong, and good or bad, that both are varying aspects of the same thing, depending on time and place and the insight of the observer. By freeing himself from preconceived notions of what is good or bad and by realizing that there are numerous intermediary stages between good and bad in each situation, man will deepen his sense of justice.

In our political thinking we often use the same kind of dichotomies. Today we witness an all-out condemnation of Communism and at the same time a trend toward relaxation and cooperation with the Soviet Union. We honor freedom and equality in the United States, and we are aghast at the violence with which a minority clings to segregation. We are a religious people, but feel that the traditional support the churches gave us is slipping. We either look upon big business as a group which brought about high efficiency and organization in a fiercely competitive struggle, or as a

118

profit-seeking class manipulating the masses with the help of
costly propaganda and fake slogans. Labor unions are viewed
either as militant and grasping organizations, or as the only
forces able to protect the rights of the workers. Caught up in
all these contrasts, Americans look for pat solutions. And as
usual extremists come forward with the easy and over-
simplified answers. Cold War? Break off diplomatic relations with Russia. Castro? Invade Cuba. Unemployment?
Give free enterprise a free rein. Taxes? Abolish progressive
taxation and let all be taxed equally. Desegregation? Enforce
state discipline. Inflation? Cut the budget, etc. The habit of
thinking in black or white leads indeed to hebetude. To overcome it requires self-discipline. Only thus will man learn
to rely on his own judgment and conscience.

Social Thinking

Having analyzed the difficulties for the average man to adapt
his thinking to the changes created by the present scientific
breakthrough, we now turn to some fields in which his
thinking has already made some significant progress. Growing
awareness of the oneness of mankind has put the accent of
social thinking on social responsibility. Social responsibility
begins at home. Man is honor bound to look after his dependents. Man is the only creature on earth whose offsprings
need such a long maturing period as to lengthen family life
until children are full-grown. In an evolutionary sense
parental care is the mainspring of love in human life.
However, man being equally responsible for his self-realization, his responsibility towards his family does not go so
far that he shall love all its members irrespective of their
intrinsic value, or sacrifice himself to the weak and in-
competent. Man's responsibility towards family and community must be dictated not by sentiment or pity alone but also by
reason and conscience. This is the basis of social thinking.

It implies that man looks after his own health and that of
his dependents, that he uses the necessary preventive care to
strengthen his own and their physical and mental resistance,
anticipates diseases and looks after his family's normal
development. There is no better way for sharpening his
foresight. No longer does man abide by the rule of "letting
nature follow its course", but he actively intervenes when-

ever his reason requires him to do so. Starting at the family level and from there extending to the community, contemporary man's responsibility reaches out to the nation and beyond that to the world community.

In Western democracies and especially in the United States a great deal of thought is given to communal problems and activities, and team spirit is growing. The churches have been helpful in supplementing their sometimes lagging moral support by social help. Americans developed a social code that promotes a smooth and friendly intercourse between one and all except in the great cities, where extreme competition breeds indifference and lawlessness. In the United States local patriotism is less pronounced than in Europe, where diversity is considered the hallmark of civilization. Neither does one encounter the jarring class differences that divide the nations of the old continent into distinct social layers. In the United States there is a spirit of live and let live that brightens American Community life.

And yet there is a flaw in the very smoothness of the American social set-up, due to the people's preference for expediency over thinking. The polite acquiescence, the easy promise and the white lie, originally meant to spare other people's sensitivities but which can shield a lack of inner conviction and of courage to voice an opinion or take a stand, are in the long run bound to have corrosive effects. In business as well as in daily intercourse a complicated network of face-saving devices, evasions and prevarications threaten man's integrity of thinking by forcing him into a colorless conformism, and also his dignity by making him forget that his word is his bond.

Apart from this, American community life has created a solid basis for good neighborliness and for mutual help in solving common problems in a cooperative spirit. While in Europe nations are formed by vertical layers of social classes, the American nation rather consists of a horizontal conglomeration of communities. This difference little affects the national concept which in the United States as well as on the old continent is still mostly predicated on power and prestige. But social thinking helped to reinforce the element of interdependence even beyond the national borders. The United States community spirit coupled to its federal form of government makes it easier for Americans to appreciate the concept of a world community than for Europeans, to whom the nation has long been the ultimate political unit.

In a fast shrinking world, social thinking has to assume global proportions the moment the individual realizes that his destiny is bound up with that of all others. The sense of responsibility this gives him demands that his goals transcend his personal interests, his community and even his national preoccupations in order to encompass the world community and, in an infinitely far-off future, even the universe. It is not accidental that in our time terrestrial man became space man. The urge to break away from our planet is proof of man's awakening to the cosmic nature of his evolution. Aware of his growing power and more active role in evolution, man is irresistibly drawn towards raising the ceiling of his thoughts ever higher.

Political Thinking

There is no field in which thinking is so steeped in prejudices, anachronisms, slogans and clichés as in politics. No field in which thought manipulation is more assiduously practised and independent thinking more impeded. On the other hand politics offer a great opportunity for introducing new ideas in the guise of reform and renewal. Politicians are roughly divided into two categories. There are those who thrive on deep-rooted traditions and prejudices and proclaim what people want to hear, giving them the security of the familiar and relieving them from the unpleasant task of thinking. Then there are those who open up new horizons and do away with preconceived ideas, outdated attitudes and stubborn routines. In the past those in the latter category used to encounter strong opposition from the conservative classes and were only able to bring home their views if conditions had become untenable. Today, helped by the realization, which is rapidly gaining ground, that nations must keep on the move to meet the omnipresent challenges and pressures, they have a better opportunity of finding a larger response. But their task remains difficult. They are opposed by an officialdom whose concern for personal security more often than not blunts their initiative and originality and to whom the introduction of new ideas seems a rather dangerous and frivolous undertaking. These bureaucrats see safety in well-tested methods, danger in the unorthodox. This, by the way, caused the frustrating experience of the last decades when a number of able men in the United States refused to assume government functions because of the difficulty of cutting across conservative mediocrity, blind conformism and the usual bureaucratic obstruction against innovations. This is coming to an end. Thoughtful and responsible men are taking over in the United States and in the West in general, replacing others who rose to the top by sheer lack of inner weight.

Such developments take time. That explains a certain disenchantment among intellectuals whose thinking outruns the time needed for overcoming prejudice and passive resistance. It is a long process before new ideas percolate to the masses. This forces the executive to exercise patience and use many levers in a number of places, giving sometimes the impression that the politician prevails in him over the statesman, whereas it is often the statesman waiting for his views to become acceptable to the people before they can be put into practice.

Nationalism

In the field of international politics people everywhere are beginning to take a different look at certain traditional concepts. One of these is the time-honored concept of nationalism. Originally invented by monarchs in order more tightly to link fiefs, vasselages, semi-independent dukedoms and satrapies or free cities to the crown, nationalism served the historic purpose of uniting populations and regions divided among themselves, giving them greater power and efficiency. Later nationalism was whipped up into a flagwaving, "my country right or wrong", aggressive emotionalism used by rulers to key up the masses in order to attain their objectives or to incite the people to war.

On the other hand nationalism gives a sense of unity and mutual protection. It evokes pride in the nation and love for it, because the individual sees in the nation an extension of himself. It also breeds intolerance and foments discord with other nations, glorifies what separates and derides what should unite them. Nationalism lost the absolute value people attached to it and, with due respect to the extreme right everywhere, both nationalism and the concept of absolute

122

sovereignty, which in the past stood out as cornerstones of political theory, are due for a thorough transformation. Here enters a question of semantics. Nationalism and patriotism are two different notions. If the value of nationalism declines this does not in the least detract from man's love for his country, which remains as strong as that for his family. It is the political, not the emotional concept which is changing. The Westerner of today senses the countless economic, cultural, scientific and human ties which transcend political boundaries. He envisages a world of merging nations, of sovereign rights subordinated to world law, and of frontiers sublimated by trade, traffic and cultural exchanges.

In the newly independent countries nationalism had at first an opposite effect. Liberated from the colonial yoke, people saw in their independence the right of being, for the first time, themselves. This incited them to ignore the unification, often artificial, imposed upon them during the past colonial rule. Long suppressed racial, religious and tribal dissensions flared up. In India, integrated under British rule, India proper and Pakistan erupted into a bloody internecine fight. After the French left, Indo-China fell apart into a number of separate states. In Indonesia strong centrifugal forces arose in many islands. Countless are the tribal wars that bring trouble and crises to the newly created African nations. All this shows that independence and nationalism are not one and the same thing. It also shows up the artificial side of present nationalism. Used by the newly independent governments as a means of diverting the people's attention from their numerous internal difficulties, nationalism became an emotional catalyst without any rational foundation. But among some of the new African nations one can already detect manifestations of political realism. Moved by considerations of common security, several of them seek some form of federation. In so doing they follow the direction of the future.

For the world is inexorably moving towards ever larger political entities. A number of states are linked into continental federations. They reached the last stage but one before a still closer coordination will permit the United Nations and other international organisations to gradually absorb more of their sovereign rights and lay a foundation for a fuller unification of the world. How this will take place cannot yet be foreseen; it is more likely to grow by way of functional cooperation than through the establishment of a world government. In any case world cooperation begins to exercise an appeal sufficiently strong to transcend strictly national considerations. Wide and fascinating world problems will in the long run evoke a greater interest than the national ones, provided that the average man's imagination can be fired to the point that he sees the whole world as his backyard. Measured against the interest Americans took fifty years ago in foreign lands, significant progress has been achieved. Interest in world unity is mounting. The dream of one world is bound to come true one day, and the sooner people get used to the idea the less disturbing the transition will be.

Nationalism is no longer the ultimate political rationale, though this may not yet be generally accepted. Though in Europe President de Gaulle is fighting a rear-guard action in favor of nationalism, Europe's final integration is but a matter of time. Inevitably the emergence of a larger entity reduces the importance of smaller units. This can be daily observed in our own federation. In the past the U.S. Constitution balanced in an exemplary way states and federal rights until, under the pressure of a mounting population and the impact of the new United States leadership of the free world, the importance of the federation began considerably to surpass that of the states. Consequently it could be expected that the members of Congress would give priority to national over local interests. What we witness, however, is an unabated action of conservative elements in favor of states' rights, and an incessant desire to cater to the parochial views of their constituencies. * If the United States is to fulfil its destiny as world leader, a first condition is that the members of Congress think of the United States in terms of a single entity that has priority over all its constituent parts. This, by the way, implies no change in our Constitution. All that is needed is for the members of Congress to declare on

---

* The attitude of a non-conservative was typified by the then Majority Leader Lyndon B. Johnson. Asked how he was going to vote on the Bricker amendment for restricting presidential powers in the field of foreign relations, his answer was that though opposed to the amendment he was nevertheless going to vote for it "because all my people in Texas want it". As related by Emmet John Hughes in "The Ordeal of Power".

their oath of office that they will put the interests of the nation above state and local interests.

Another example of clinging to traditional political thinking occurred shortly before the conclusion of the nuclear test ban agreement. By now most people realize that some sort of cooperation with the Soviet Union is necessary to steer away from the Cold War. But on the eve of the agreement the whole gamut of anti-Communist slogans was again run. * In Congress there was a good deal of criticism, some of the members being opposed to any deal with the Russians, others to the United States abandoning its freedom of nuclear testing, and still others wanting a number of safeguards written into the agreement. However, when it came to voting, a large majority declared itself in favor of the treaty. Which may well prove that even the conservative members of Congress begin to share the keen sense of the majority of Americans that the United States has to keep working for an ever closer relationship with the rest of the world.

Sovereignty

If nationalism is becoming outdated, so is absolute sovereignty. In its original sense that a state is entirely free to act as it wants to, it no longer exists. Every treaty restricts a state's freedom of action. As every state concluded countless treaties and agreements with other states and is bound by these as by its own constitution, the decision to subordinate sovereignty to a code of international law would merely extend an already existing situation. To put this principle into operation requires an international tribunal to administer

---

* U.S. banks urged buying U.S. bonds "in this time of national peril" in order to safeguard "our most precious heritage which is threatened by forces more powerful, more resourceful, more destructive than at any time of our history". The annual Governors' Conference insisted on continuing at this very moment an, in itself useful, educational campaign about the dangers of Communism. Professors of Political Science wrote letters to editors criticizing the President for advocating an easing of tensions with our Communist foes instead of denouncing their dangerous machinations and extolling the virtues of our system of freedom.

international law and an international police to enforce it. To enlarge the competence of the World Court would be a first step; to create such an international force able to police the world and exercise sanctions, without which no law is enforceable, is the next step. The United Nations can play an important role in this transformation, provided that the great powers find ways and means of mitigating their right of veto. To cling to an absolute right of veto is tantamount to upholding absolute sovereignty.

War and Peace

Under the impact of the balance of terror our thinking about war changed, as we mentioned before. Nuclear war, defeating its own purpose, gradually fades out of the range of practical contingencies. Brush and local wars—as well as revolutions may still for a long time remain the means for changing existing equilibria, but they will be used with greater circumspection than before and in all probability remain localized. The days are past when wars were the prime movers in relationships between nations, and peace the period necessary to generate new energy for the next fighting bout. Communist leaders, too, rationalized war. Moscow uses it mainly as a psychological lever and Peking as a means of keeping up the nation's "face" and distracting attention from internal difficulties.

Our thinking about peace is also changing. During times immemorial, peace was looked upon as a breathing spell between wars. More recently peace was called utopian, not so much on account of the old saying that man with his predatory instincts will always fight as long as he lives, but because of the belief that an untenable social or international status-quo can only be changed through war or revolution.

Today, under democratic rule, political changes can be obtained differently. While in the past the only means of overthrowing the existing order of the mighty and powerful was through bloody upheavals, at present it can be brought down by majority vote. However, on the international scene little has been changed. As under the Pax Romana and the Pax Britannica, the principal powers continue to impose their decisions on other nations. Efforts to introduce a majority rule in world affairs cannot succeed as long as the present discrepancy in military and industrial power between nations continues to exist. Power equality is not likely to be achieved until all nations unite in continental federations. Then the road will be open for collabokation on equal terms and for a peaceful review of outdated treaties and situations. Such changes require a feat of rationalization which is a far cry from our present emotional attitude. It will take mankind quite some time to sublimate its emotions and resist demagogic appeals, but it cannot hurt to think this over and clarify our thoughts in anticipation.

What remains a utopia is the peace of the pacifists and their unilateral disarmament. Multilateral disarmament is a different question. It becomes more and more desirable to put an end to the armament race. Not merely to avoid nuclear war, but on account of all the energy and capital which today is invested in arms and which can be put to better use. But disarmament is impossible without an end to mutual suspicion, and this cannot be overcome without more cooperation in a number of fields between East and West. Peace cannot be achieved by abolition of arms : peace results from a meeting of minds, from a general agreement among the powers to live up to a common purpose. Peace demands seeing the world as one.

Freedom

A political concept which seems immutable, but nevertheless also changes with the times is freedom. Freedom is a many-sided concept. It can mean obtaining the right over one's own body, gaining the right of indirectly taking part in the government or the right to enjoy a fair share in the fruits of one's labor. Freedom's only limitations lie in the freedom of others or in the vague borderline between freedom and license. All during man's history people have been prepared to give their life for obtaining freedom, but once procured it is taken for granted and given little thought. Freedom is a word constantly used by statesmen all over the world. Its meaning is seldom elucidated, because it is deemed self-evident. But is it?

Freedom carries different appeals at different periods and should therefore be occasionally re-interpreted. The last time this happened was during the war, when the Atlantic Charter added freedom from fear and want to the other freedoms. This somewhat negative interpretation did not go to the heart of the concept, which, in its wider, evolutionary sense, demands the right to free and unfettered thought, permitting the questioning of any opinion or dogma and the right to proclaim one's own views without risking being punished or ostracized, unless one transgresses a law or commits treasonable sedition. Freedom today more and more appears as the right to change. The right to use one's own insight in preparing any change deemed indispensable for the advance of mankind.

In the course of our study we remarked that freedom seems to have lost some of its appeal. This may be due to the fact that in parts of the world man's individual freedom evokes less sympathy than the urge for solidarity, but it is also caused by the free world's lack of regularly adapting freedom to ever more rapidly changing conditions. Even in the West, cradle of liberty, freedom has lost some of its luster. It is hardly a generation ago that Germans surrendered their freedom to the Nazis without so much as a thought. It is true that in 1933 it was only fifteen years since the Weimar Republic had discarded the last remnants of feudalism. But even in the old-established democracies the cynical remark could be heard in times of economic crisis that freedom does not provide bread. As to the Communists, they fell from Tsarist autocracy into Communist tyranny and never knew any freedom except during the short Kerenski interval. Their "ersatz" freedom has nothing to do with the real thing, but the fact that the Communists effected the substitution without raising more of an outcry in the rest of the world should make us think.

In the West, freedom has connotations of great traditions and a glorious heritage. But it no longer represents the indomitable urge to constantly rejuvenate its institutions, attitudes and thinking and to incite others to do likewise. It is this failure to re-interpret freedom which deprives the West of a sense of purpose. Granted the wisdom of constitutional safeguards that slow down changes in order to protect against temporary bursts of enthusiasm or demagoguery, this does not justify a basic disinclination towards change. Looking a little closer, what we see is often the opposite of the right to change. We detect a pattern of traditions and attitudes to which society forces man to conform even if they go against his convictions. Intense pressure to adhere to moral and intellectual viewpoints acceptable to the majority of the cautious and the slow, gentler but still insistent pressure not to question existing beliefs, demands by political, business and other leaders to stick to certain well-defined attitudes and, finally, the desire to "belong" to a group and not to differ from the average form serious obstacles to independent thinking. It is this more than anything else which prevents man from finding and fulfilling himself, and it is in this respect that freedom should find a new expression and realization. With the greatest regard for experience and traditions, because they made us what we are, we should not accept them as unbreakable rules. And they definitely should not prevent us from seeking for new truths and occasionally revising our scale of values. If our people, if all the peoples of the world, would realise that the tremendous changes around us, caused by the breakthrough of science, are but a beginning, a mere shadow of what is to follow once man fully develops his faculties and if they would understand that to do this man must be free in his thinking, then freedom will assume a new magic.

A hundred years ago Lincoln gave to this country a new birth of freedom by re-uniting it in liberty. Today we do not need a rebirth of freedom in this nation—though segregation still prevents all citizens from gaining full freedom—but our task is to give a new birth of freedom to the world. For Lincoln's concern that freedom should not disappear from the face of this earth has become a basic demand of evolution, and therefore of the survival of the human race.

We know that everyone's freedom is limited by the freedom of others. In the past these others were our neighbors and countrymen; today they are all those with whom we are in contact all over the world, our allies and our friends, those who look for our help and protection, those for whom we assumed responsibility and finally those with whom we disagree or whom we distrust and with whom we nevertheless share a common destiny. In fact these others are all the peoples of the world. Today freedom means to forge a bond of liberty with all of them. This new view on freedom contains an element of collective responsibility and as such could be a kind of freedom which Communism can understand. Such liberty holds the key to a world of reason in which man can learn to overcome trials and afflictions such as poverty, disease, fear and other tribulations and in which, infinitely slowly but surely, man will replace the rule of blind chance by the power of his mind. To improve his mind man must probe deeper and deeper and always be open to new ideas. True originality demands real freedom, and it is only through originality of mind that mankind can progress.

To the free countries, freedom of thought and the right to openly express it are an absolute necessity. Without it no man can produce the inventiveness, the power of synthesis and vision to face new situations and penetrate new worlds. Without it he cannot succeed in reaching the inner core of other men and establish that world-wide cooperation of minds that by sheer force of multiplication is alone able to overcome the formidable difficulties which mankind will encounter on the ascent towards the next stage of its evolution.

To the Communist regimes independent thinking is anathema. New and unorthodox ideas are deemed "dangerous" in a closed society and prejudicial to the leading group. Yet the Communists know as well as we do that no human institution is permanent and that there is none that does not require change. They equally know that changes are brought about by foresight and the creative genius of the individual, and they must realize that countries whose choice of such individuals is severely restricted must, in the end, lose out against nations with a quasi unlimited choice.

A strange contradiction has emerged between the free and Communist worlds. In the free world the freedom of the individual has become inseparable from his responsibility towards others. Though capitalism was originally greedy, the Western society of today is increasingly aware of its responsibility for all. The individual is taught to assume responsibilities in his community, in the nation and even in the world. In Communism it is solely the collectivity which is responsible for all, and Communism thus deprives itself of the educational value of giving responsibility for others to the individual. But in a world which accepts the oneness of mankind, Communism will finally have to recognize the necessity of not only having all carry the responsibility for each, but also each the responsibility for all. And so both freedom and individual responsibility are bound to emerge one day under Communist regimes. Ultimately the Com-

munists, too, will have to admit that the distinctive characteristics of human nature are freedom and man's consciousness
of and responsibility towards all others.

Thinking in Terms of the Future

Before concluding this chapter we have to deal with the kind
of thinking which is resolutely turned to the future, and which
in the long run is certain to supersede the still predominant
habit of thinking in terms of the present and the past. As we
saw, to think in the past means to think according to established patterns, to take things for granted and to seek
security in well-tried views of others without investigating
original approaches of one's own. People who think in this
way cling tenaciously to their national traditions, which, in
the United States, means to the American way of life, inherited
from ancestors who in their days, however, <u>did</u> have the
courage to break with the past and plunge headlong into an
unknown future.

Those who think ahead do not "a priori" accept all "axiomatic" truths. They think independently and, beyond the scope
of their daily work, their community and their nation, in
global dimensions. They see in the extremes of poverty and
wealth, and in social, racial, political and economic inequalities and discriminations the main cause of world-wide
tensions and explosions. By realizing man's place in the
scheme of things, they succeed in gaining a more detached
view. They believe that much depends on man's mind, that
those who have reached a sufficient thought capacity can see
light where others still see darkness, recognize order where
others see chaos, or enter into the spirit of things where
others remain hopelessly entangled in matter. They recognize evil, suffering and injustice as being caused by nature's
blind groping and the arbitrariness of chance or as the result
of evolution's own growing pains, because every progress is
inevitably accompanied by a great effort of labor and suffering.
They trust that man can be progressively instrumental in
mitigating some of these negative aspects. They begin to see
themselves as active participants in evolution. At long last
cut adrift from the Stone Age, these men have definitely
entered the Age of Reason.

Changes in Our Thinking

The tendency to think in terms of the future is not yet general, but everywhere men arise who resolutely turn to it. Coming from all walks of life, they recognize each other by their affinity of thought. Under their guidance the up and coming generation learns to sharpen its perception and inventiveness, and to increase its foresight. This generation may finally bring forth the end of the struggle between religion and science. It may come forward with a synthesis in which there is no longer room for contradiction between science and faith and in which, even if the "why" remains unanswerable, the "how" will be understood one day without an appeal to the supernatural. Thinking in terms of the future will replace fear, frustration and doubt by insight, understanding and self-reliance.

Many a reader may object that this chapter is an exercise in cold intellectualism and devoid of feeling. He may ask if man does not have a heart besides his mind and whether the heart does not reveal the best in man. What about love and beauty, music and all other forms of art, what about creative inspiration and achievement, and also the throbbing passions, the rip-roaring zest for living, the abandon in battle, the overflowing vitality? What about God's mercy and His Providence, man's rebellion against injustice and cruelty, and life's lack of logic, and the irony of fate? Above all what about man's soul? Do not man's strongest and finest emotions stem from his heart and not from his mind?

We do not raise this problem in order to present an "apologia". Everyone who looks ahead must be prepared for criticism and even outright rejection of his ideas by those disinclined to leave the safety of accepted and approved views. If we touch upon these matters it is to express a conviction, grown with the years, that man's mind is the greatest gift which God has bestowed on him and that to construct a duality between man's mind and man's soul is contrary to all which can be observed in nature.

Man's mind represents to date the pinnacle of evolution. It is his only instrument through which he becomes conscious of and can rationalize knowledge, art, morality and religion, the instrument which permits him to conceive and measure the depth of beauty and harmony, to approach the mysterious with awe and veneration, and also to overcome his instincts, fears and superstitions and, to a degree, the rule of fate.

It is the instrument through which universe and spirit reveal themselves to him, directly and without any interpretation of dogma. Man's mind is the instrument through which he probes his conscience and through which he can gradually liberate himself from matter and become conscious of God.

Others see man's intelligence as opposed to his faith and sentiment. According to them, man's materialism results from his cerebrations which invented Communism in the slums of degradation. They say that faith is a matter of grace, as if man's mind is not also a mark of grace. This duality between faith and mind has been instilled in man during millennia, but time and again he reacted to this encroachment on his liberty. He wanted to decide and understand for himself. It is only when he is at a loss to comprehend that man resorts to symbols, of which the countless deities of days long past bear witness. Man's soul is such a symbol. Its transcendental nature defies rationalization. It covers the undefinable. The more his perception grows, the less becomes man's need to refer to it. Man can only advance by searching for truth. And truth is what is within the grasp of his understanding at a given period of his evolution.

Here then lies the answer to our quest as far as we can today become aware of it. The more man's knowledge advances the less he will be in need of his present symbolism. *
As man learns to replace sentimentality and emotionalism by sentiment and emotion, sublimating both by the rationalizing power of his mind, his worship of the all-pervading Spirit will widen and deepen. Cultivation of the mind has become the highest form of religion.

With greater reassurance and purpose man is thinking ahead. Aware of the forces of evolution he prepares himself to acquire the foresight and power of guidance he is called upon to exercise. Provided that those who turn to the future increase in numbers—as they seem to do—and providing that they succeed in educating the coming generation in their way of thinking, there is reason to be optimistic as to man's chances of overcoming the present crisis in his evolution. An objective survey of the present situation reveals some

---

* In his further evolution man will undoubtedly be faced with immense new regions of ignorance which will require new symbols, but these will be of a different nature.

133

encouraging facts. There <u>is</u> a growing consensus in the world that nuclear war is folly, war <u>is</u> already fought by psychological rather than military weapons; peaceful use of nuclear energy on earth and in space <u>has</u> already fired man's imagination everywhere; and the Cold War <u>has</u> lost some of its violence and militancy.

Our survival from the present crisis need not be a miracle as Lord Bertram Russell wrote, nor an act of Providence, but it is more likely to be the work of man become conscious of the obligations which reason imposes on him. Man's mind is the decisive factor. This means that pious hope and prayers no longer suffice. Man has to apply himself with all his sagacity and foresight, knowing, as President Kennedy said in his inaugural speech, "that here on earth God's work must be truly our own".

Chapter XII

PROBLEMS OF THE FUTURE

Closer acquaintance with the modern theory of evolution not only changes man's thinking, it also helps him to envisage a number of new problems in a new spirit. These problems no longer loom on the horizon, they are here in our midst as a result of the recent unequalled advance of science. Every new day, so to say, brings new problems which are so different from those of the past and so all-embracing as to require a new, global, logic. As this logic equally applies to the solution of the political impasse this book is dealing with, a few of these future problems are examined in this chapter.

Thinking Machines

One of the most typical products of the scientific break-through and a striking example of what man's inventiveness can achieve, are the electronic machines which are literally man's brainchild, which possess a brain of their own, a life-span, the capacity not only of correcting some of their errors but in certain instances also of re-creation. So ingenious are some of them that they brought into being the new science of cybernetics which attempts to explain the nature of the human brain by comparing it to complex electronic computers. With the exception of creative thinking, these machines can perform a number of human mental functions from forecasting an election to playing a game of checkers.

These machines have already become indispensable in many fields of science and industry such as astronomy and mathematics, atomic structure and nuclear processes, aero-nautics, statistics, etc., and are destined to play a decisive role in man's progress. From calculating machines they have become machines with a capacity for deductive reasoning and therefore able to control an automatic factory. Next machines were built with an adaptive capacity which are able to decide on alternative courses and are thus, in the real sense, thinking machines. These machines not only relieve man of long and tedious calculations or of a number of physical and mechanical jobs by their automative capacity, they also can free man's mind of the necessity of analyzing certain contingencies or weighing certain decisions. Such machines are today in current use. No modern business, no planning can be conducted without computers. Just as automobiles and aeroplanes became artificial improvements of man's limbs, computers will in the near future become the indispensable extensions of man's brain and memory.

Electronic machines are not only affecting the individual by lightening his routine tasks, they also introduce to man everywhere the same kind of instrument for conducting research and planning ahead, and are thus likely to exercise a converging influence, achieving all over the world the metamorphosis of homo sapiens into the organizational man. The French scientist Pierre Bertaux remarks in his book on the "Mutation of Mankind" * that it well lies within tomorrow's possibilities that a sophisticated electronic machine could predict the outcome of a war between the U.S. and U.S.S.R. and therefore make it superfluous. He adds that this not only makes it important that both sides are precisely informed about each other's armed strength, but that it also provides a decisive argument against the emergence of a third or further nuclear power. For if the outcome of a war between two powers is predictable, the involvement of a third or fourth power would make computations so intricate that even a machine could no longer solve them.

The question has been asked whether his increasing dependence on machines will not make contemporary man still more vulnerable than he already is. Such concern seems to be borne out by the disrupting effect a power shortage can have on life in a big city such as New York. But this is not necessarily the case for the kind of machines which man uses as thinking antennae provided that they have a built-in source of energy and are not dependent on an outside power station. In any case there can be no doubt that man is going to provide himself with more and more machines to extend or supple-

---

* Pierre Bertaux, "Mutation der Menschheit, Diagnosen und Prognosen", a book written in German by a Frenchman.

ment his limbs, sense organs, thinking capacities and memo-
ory, and that his increased potentialities will, in turn,
further sharpen his mind.

Planning

Planning on a national and even global scale is one of the
problems which increasingly demand man's attention and
concentration. Because planning forms the keystone of
Marxist economy, there is still a certain resistance against
it in the United States. It would be absurd to say that Americans do not plan. From their earliest history when they had
to conquer a continent, they were forced to plan ahead. As a
matter of fact, organizational planning in business is a specific
American trait. It shows up in market analyses, consumer
tests, opinion research, manufacturing and sales planning
and in numerous other ways. But planning remains prepon-
derantly a private affair, and overall government planning is
still being equated by business with government interference
in free enterprise.

Yet planning and forethought on a national and even global
scale are elementary in an age of rationalization. Under today's population pressure, and in a world economy that
directly influences our markets and, moreover, partly depends
on our help, government planning can no longer be avoided.
All our allies have a certain degree of overall economic
planning and the question even arises whether our slower
economic growth in comparison with theirs is not due to our
insufficient planning. In France, planning was worked out by
Jean Monnet after the war, and methodically carried out after
de Gaulle came to power. It is based on cooperation between
the government, an official Planning Board, the Economic and
Social Council, 300 "ad hoc" commissions composed of top
business and labor leaders and officials who together decide
about the annual growth rate of the economy ($5\frac{1}{2}\%$ for 1963)
and the production and expansion rate of all its sectors. This
French planning sharply departs from the American competitive view, but offers the advantage of a well balanced
simultaneous growth. Approved projects obtain low-interest
capital from the Banque de France, spontaneous ventures have
to find money on the more expensive open market. In Germany, government planning comes less to the fore. To begin

with, this is the first time in its history that Germany has switched from a strongly protectionist to a free economy. But apart from that there exists a highly organized cooperation between management and labor which facilitates integrated planning. In both France and Germany, but also in Italy, Austria, the Netherlands, Switzerland and Scandinavia planning had remarkable results. In the decade from 1950-60 their respective G.N.P. and productivity rose in Germany 7.4% and 5%, in France 4.3% and 3.9%, in Italy 5.7% and 4%, in Austria 6.2% and 5.7%, in the Netherlands 5% and 3.6% and in Sweden 3.5% and 3.3%, against in the United States 2.9% and 1.9%.

Actually the United States also introduced a considerable margin of overall planning. This is unavoidable in a country which in 1973 will have a population of 226 million against 190 million today and a G.N.P. of 900 billion dollars against 600 billion in 1963. Government planning is necessary considering that the Defense Department spends over 50 billion dollars a year with direct repercussions on large segments of the economy and on employment. Overall planning is also needed to mitigate the results of automation, to regulate agricultural production with its reactions on the home and foreign markets, to look after the balance of payments and, finally to organize our foreign help and commitments.

An increase in general planning is likely to have its repercussions on American business, with its emphasis on teamwork. It is hardly to be expected that large corporations operating in similar or related fields and faced with problems of today's magnitude would not establish a measure of cooperation. Accustomed to cooperating with labor organizations whose interests are often opposed, it is no wonder if they try to do the same with companies on their side of the table. The day may not be far off when cooperation is partly to replace competition in business. This becomes possible as soon as consumers see fit to unite for the defense of their interests into a third group besides management and labor, whereupon anti-trust legislation can be adjusted. And so planning is likely to change American capitalism.

Planning is the essence of every economic activity, national and worldwide, as a result of the growing convergence of all nations. Capitalist planning will always differ from Marxist planning in that it gives more consideration to individual initiative, but the idea that capitalism could operate without overall planning is an illusion. In a world in which man becomes conscious of his ability partly to guide his and mankind's destiny, and in which his foresight plays a decisive role, planning has become a must. We previously remarked that electronic machines promote planning on a world scale because they operate uniformly. This offers the additional advantage of facilitating international cooperation in world problems.

In this section only economic planning has been mentioned, but it goes without saying that the reasons which militate for it equally apply to political thinking. One had only to watch the activities of a Khrushchev to realize how far ahead he prepared his moves. A de Gaulle carefully proceeded by first carrying through the constitutional changes which France needed to overcome its past paralysis. Then he liquidated the Algerian war, which sapped its manpower and vitality, and because this was a severe blow to France's prestige, he balanced it out by raising France's grandeur on the international scene. Hence his rapprochement with Germany, necessary to regain leadership in Europe, his opposition to American policy in order to bolster Europe's self-assurance, and his step-by-step efforts to raise France's influence in Africa, the Far-East, Latin-America and, tomorrow, Soviet Russia.

The kind of political planning incumbent on the United States is dealt with in Chapter XIV on American Foreign Policy.

Automation

Electronic machines were preceded by the introduction of mechanical appliances and devices in the household. Currently regarded abroad as typifying American materialism, they achieve the opposite result of helping overcome a good deal of drudgery and giving, especially to women, more time for occupation with matters of the mind. They brought automation to the home. Electronics gave a boost to automation by extending it from the home to the manufacturing plant and providing the possibility of running entire factories by remote control. This is going to cause a major economic and social upheaval in the American way of life.

There is, to begin with, the problem of over-production.

Problems of the Future

How is the American economy going to absorb a considerably increased production of goods when, in the next decade, the G.N.P. is to rise by 50 per cent and the individual's income by no more than 25 per cent? Economists arrived at the conclusion that this would make it necessary to provide the average citizen with a basic income sufficient to purchase the goods produced by automatic factories, and this irrespective of his work and earning capacity. But then automation would bring the American citizen into an impasse. If the incentive for earning an income disappears, the bottom falls out of our capitalistic society. If the challenge to produce goes, so does our scale of values. This poses the question of what the American citizen must strive for once he attains affluence.

The second problem which automation raises is one of unemployment. In 1963 automation cost the United States forty thousand jobs a week. There is likely to be a shift from blue to white collar workers, but this will not solve the problem. If as many men would be needed to build and service electronic machines as those whom automation eliminates, there would be no sense in automation. Automation is going to force countless people to seek a better education as a means of survival. Consequently the average worker is due for a remarkable metamorphosis. With increasing technological education the worker of today is becoming the technician of tomorrow, today's technician tomorrow's engineer, and the engineer of today the managerial leader and perhaps the statesman of the future. The question is what to do with the millions of unskilled workers.

The answers to both problems of over-production and unemployment have to be found by transposing them from the American to the world scene. If as a result of automation the United States can no longer absorb its production, it seems logical to channel into the world the extra purchasing power which economists destined to our own people. Such an increase of global purchasing power, especially in the poor nations, could be achieved by foreign aid, capital investments and government secured loans. This, incidentally, would also benefit the United States. In such manner the competitive challenge would be kept alive for the American citizen, and his productive capacities put to the service of mankind. In the process, increasing numbers of unemployed workers could find occupation abroad. Today these thoughts might look chimerical, tomorrow they will be self-evident. In the meantime the main thing is to keep the national economy going until it adapts itself to world dimensions.

Unemployment

Let us return to the problem of unemployment in the United States as it is likely to develop in the next years. At the time of writing, the United States has a permanent unemployment of more than 4.5 million workers or over 5.5 per cent of the labor force of 76 million, resulting from structural changes caused by the technological advance. It consists mainly of colored people, whose unemployment is based on the myth of inequality of the races, of youngsters who lacked the time or opportunity to learn a trade, of women, and in general of unskilled workers. Automation will further increase unemployment, and this calls for a re-appraisal and transformation of our economic set-up. This problem cannot be solved by the Keynesian remedy of government spending and pump priming in order to artificially inject purchasing power, for it was meant to overcome full-blown economic crises and not structural maladjustments. Even if today the administration surpasses Keynes' recipe by cutting down taxes in order to increase purchasing power during a booming economy, this cannot solve the unemployment problem. * And still less if the major powers should one day agree to gradual disarmament. If this were to happen, the huge injections of money resulting from arms expenditures would slowly dry up and a labor force of twelve million men would have to be gradually re-allocated. Some of these men can be used in large public works for fighting erosion, flood control, irrigation, etc. though the advent of nuclear power reduces the number of men required today for such undertakings. New opportunities

---

* The notion of a balanced budget—which such tax cuts render still more difficult—is one of the over-simplified slogans of our age. It may have a certain appeal, but this does not alter the fact that a budget in the red, though prejudicial to the rich, benefits the workers because it creates a measure of inflation which causes a redistribution of wealth, and is not dangerous as long as it remains proportionate to the increase of the G.N.P.

for employment in the world of tomorrow lie in the field of service industries, professionally organized social services for the home, children's care, hospitals and the like. The greatest opportunity arises in an unexpected field, namely education and research, which will grow at the same pace as man's mind develops. But as the training of personnel for producing teachers and scientists requires a lengthy preparation, this poses another difficult problem. It must be solved because the survival of our civilization depends on it, and a major effort to enlarge our educational system should be the first move towards solving the worsening crisis in unemployment. *

As automation spreads, and machines become further perfected and men familiarized with their use, the entire image of our world will change. And this is likely to happen before the end of the century. Then a relatively small force of workers will be able to handle the entire American production apparatus. Man's main occupation will more and more switch to research, science and exploration. No longer the world alone, space also will absorb a good deal of man's energies. The general trend will be one of intensified mechanization of the material side of life next to growing spiritualization, i.e. the main accent will be transferred from the brawn to the brain. The stage will be set for the spirit to gradually overcome matter.

Leisure

By shortening working hours, automation is already changing the life of the workers. The full impact will not be felt until a four day work week is reached, but then leisure will also pose a problem. The problem of what the individual is going to do with so much free time on his hands. This does not apply to the managerial and professional classes, the business executives, doctors, professors, lawyers and self-

---

* A temporary expedient might consist in asking men and women who, though having reached the retirement age, are still qualified to teach and sufficiently elastic for gauging the problems of the future, to come to the rescue. The enrolment of older citizens can only be temporary, for otherwise it would defeat the purpose of creating new jobs in the future.

employed, who are likely to continue their self-imposed sixty or more hour week. But for the others the question is how to utilize for the common benefit the formidable amount of potential energy released from regular work. The problem will further gain in importance when the retirement age becomes even more advanced. After catering to his personal and family needs, applying himself to his hobbies, to sports and to adult education, man will want to use his newly won leisure for more creative purposes. Some may find an outlet in art, others may go into research, without pay, for science's sake. A great deal of energy is likely to be channeled into typically American community activities, not only in our country, but across the borders in a number of projects in which our growing sense of responsibility towards the rest of the world can express itself. In this way the pessimism voiced by psychiatrists and sociologists about the psychological danger of leisure can be obviated, for it is caused by their too parochial approach to the problem within the confines of U.S. economy. While our national economy is developing into a regional bloc economy, and finally in a world economy, a glut on the market or unemployment can be overcome by channeling part of our production and part of our labor force to foreign countries as engineers, technicians, teachers for school and business, supervisors, social helpers, etc. The trail blazed by the Peace Corps is likely to be followed by a number of energetic men and women prepared to shoulder some of the world-wide responsibilities of the United States, which, whether it likes it or not, has become the leading power of the world.

Capitalism

As long as capitalism operates mainly in a national society, certain ground rules and a certain social equilibrium can be maintained. Especially if it has the elasticity of American capitalism for introducing necessary changes. Its erstwhile extreme competition was mitigated when it was realized that higher wages create an army of new consumers. Its protectionist character could be changed when it became possible with the help of technology to compete against foreign producers paying lower wages. Nevertheless it is becoming more difficult to maintain the high Western living standards

143

in the midst of a world of poverty, especially since the various national economies have become increasingly interdependent. For when national economies expand into a world economy, sooner or later a movement of global redistribution of wealth must set in. In the end, improved living conditions and increased purchasing power will benefit business everywhere. This will raise the expectations of millions of have-nots, quiet their distress, dampen their revolutionary ardor and create a more relaxed atmosphere.

This will change American economic thinking. Already social considerations play an increasingly important role in American business. A managerial class, no longer burdened by the acquisitiveness of direct ownership, shows growing concern not only for the personnel of its corporations but equally for the public at large. Profits no longer are the sole motivation of business, and the status of wealth and protection of free enterprise against government interference have lost some of their importance. American businessmen may still grumble about government intervention; nevertheless they know that it has become unavoidable under the population pressure and growing inequality between the world's poor and the wealthy. They know that we are on the long and difficult road towards a single world economy, a road from which there is no return, and they reluctantly gave up thinking in terms of a national economy alone. This implies that the days are past when better know-how, organization, production and distribution can benefit one economy to the detriment of others.

Capitalism is like the bloodstream in the human body. Parts into which it does not penetrate die off. This applies not only to a nation, but to the whole world. Until recently capital went where it could earn the highest profits. But under the growing sense of responsibility for less- and under-developed nations, the United States and other Western countries supply capital where it brings no or insignificant dividends. Laudable as this is, in the long run it is not the right approach. If a wealthy country of the West provides private or government capital to a newly independent country, this creates a kind of dependency which is too reminiscent of former colonial relationships.

In our capitalistic world it has been the rule that in all areas in which capital investment could yield no dividends,

144

such as education, health, pure scientific research, etc., it is the government which supplies the capital needs. Or to express it differently, it is the community, because the government obtains its funds through taxation. On the analogy of this it would be preferable if not one country but the community of nations were to supply underdeveloped countries with their capital requirements. This would have the advantage of eliminating colonial sensibilities and also of necessitating the "haves" of the world to coordinate their help in order to avoid working at cross purposes. As Soviet Russia belongs to the "haves" it would have the added advantage of inducing the two ideological opponents to cooperate instead of obstructing each other in the field of international aid.

Capitalism cannot escape the iron rule of change and neither can Communism. Something is likely to emerge which bears little resemblance to classic capitalism or dialectic Marxism. Under the same impact that makes humanity converge, capitalism and Communism will also converge towards certain forms of economic cooperation. Gazing further into the future, once the crassest poverty has been overcome, prosperity will become more general as new markets are opened as a result of better global understanding and cooperation.

Poverty

If such a stately and ancient institution as the Catholic Church became aware, in the person of the late Pope John XXIII, the kindly renovator whose heart went out to the needs of the poor all over the world, that reforms are a condition of survival for every kind of organization or society, it is not surprising that a dynamic democracy, such as the American finds it necessary continuously to rejuvenate itself. The administration's decision to wage an all-out war against poverty within the United States reveals its realism.

Poverty is the greatest of social evils, and the breeding ground of physical, moral and mental degradation, of sickness, prostitution, juvenile delinquency, despair and of any kind of subversive political experiment because the poor have nothing to lose and have only to gain by revolutionary upheavals. Extreme poverty in a country results from the lack of social responsibility and economic organization and from

145

the gross indifference of the wealthy classes who fail to see that the time is fast running out when they can keep their destiny apart from that of others.

In an affluent society it is not easy to recognize the various aspects of poverty, especially since social security and other social provisions take a heavy load off the individual's shoulders. Our system is different from the Communist one, where the state practically assures everyone's basic needs, because we believe in the individual's opportunity to look after himself. But in our society many lack that opportunity and our system must therefore be revised. There is the poverty of the Negro population which is discriminated against racially and economically, there is the poverty of the young people whose health and education are neglected as appears from the large percentage of rejects by the army, of the poor farmers whose share in the agricultural price support is infinitesimal, of the insufficiently educated, the women and such groups as the migrant workers who are plainly exploited. Our poverty is only relative compared to that of other countries. Half of our "poor" people still possess a car, radio or T.V., but unless the various pockets of poverty, especially among the colored population, are removed, we cannot successfully attack the infinitely more complex problem of world poverty. There our contribution must not only consist in material aid but in the shining example of a society which, by the strength of its free institutions, has been able to free at least its own part of the world of the evil of poverty.

Population Explosion

The world population, which in the year 1650 amounted to 500 million and in 1750 to 750 million, rose to one billion in 1850 and since then in a steep curve to nearly three billion today. *
At present the world population increases by fifty-five million a year. Should this continue at the same rate, the world will have six billion people at the end of the century, and after a few more centuries there will only be standing room on earth. The problem surpasses man's understanding and defies a

* The U.S. population doubled during the last 50 years and is now around the 190 million mark.

solution. Besides giving him a feeling of immobilization and suffocation, as in certain overcrowded areas in Europe where a single, unbroken suburbia absorbs all open spaces, the population explosion presents definite dangers.

It deepens the rift between the haves and have-nots, causes unrest and heightens tensions which could lead to a catastrophic overflow of Chinese hordes into Siberia, Indian ones into the Middle East or similar outbreaks leading to war. It prevents a number of underdeveloped countries from even maintaining the bare subsistence level on which their people live. For these countries cannot absorb the yearly addition of millions to their economy with the result that the present individual income, which varies in some of these countries from five to twenty dollars per month, is being further lowered. The hundreds of millions of dollars which they receive in foreign aid and investments—and which amounted to sixty billion dollars during the past decade— barely suffice to maintain the existing average living standards in these countries. On the other hand living standards in the more privileged countries continuously rise, further widening the gap between poor and rich.

The population explosion involves other dangers. Spiralling populations everywhere are likely to use up the world's reserves of raw materials in a comparatively short period, taxing to the utmost the inventiveness of coming generations to replace them. This does not mean that a solution will not be found, for man has hitherto always been able to extricate himself from difficult situations. But meanwhile, conditions may deteriorate to the point of greatly impeding or even preventing a rational approach to the problem.

Until the nineteenth century three of the four horsemen of the Apocalypse, war, famine and pestilence, were able to hold the world's population in check. The sudden rise came during the past century, when after reaching the one billion mark in 1830, it rose to two billion in 1930 and three billion today. It looks today as if man will have to reduce voluntarily the birth rate. Foresight in the planning of a family was, in the past, restricted to some sophisticated Western countries. In the rest of the world, children were being conceived at random without regard to their chances of survival in an over-populated world on account of the physiological in-compatibility of the parents in blood types and other causes for hereditary diseases. Today it seems inevitable that the emotional aspect of sex will be subjected to more rational and social considerations. Man's growing sense of responsibility towards mankind and his progress in science lead towards birth control. The Catholic Church, long opposed to it, nowadays sanctions a measure of birth regulation. Sweden and Japan made a successful beginning with birth control; in Japan the birth rate fell by fifty per cent during the past years. Even in Red China, birth control was started in 1956, but then abandoned when Peking needed all available manpower for the "great leap forward". When this failed, birth control was again taken up in 1962 because the feeding of a yearly excess of fifteen million people proved impossible. Now the government proclaims that "medical advancement has long put the initiative of child bearing in our hands. Therefore we should adopt the same serious and careful attitude towards child bearing as the one we adopt towards work and study". The problem lies mainly with the women, but as the chances are that birth control will be more successful in the sophisticated West than among the prolific races of Africa and Asia, we run the risk that the have-nots will further increase and the haves decrease. In a world in which the rule of law has not yet displaced the rule of force this is dangerous.

On the other hand and apart from all this, there is no way of knowing whether the sudden population increase was not necessary: (1) in order to hasten mankind's compression into a single organism, and (2) in order to produce the density of thought waves needed to create the sphere of common thinking which, in turn, accelerates the perfection of man's mind. Should this be the case—as it may well be—then the increase of population may automatically reach its point of saturation, man's fertility diminish* and, as Teilhard believes, the movement of mankind's extension be followed by one of contraction.

Genetics

Even more difficult and hazardous than intervention in the birth rate would be interference in man's genetic build up. In view of his irrepressible curiosity to discover nature's secrets, there is every likelihood that he will sooner or later

---

* In the animal world there are a number of examples of reduced fertility resulting from overcrowded environments.

148

experiment in genetics and try to improve on natural selection. It would indeed be to the advantage of the human race if man could have healthier descendants by a judicious choice of mating partners and, as microbiology further advances, by an artificial stimulation of positive mutations and a prevention of regressive ones.

In the field of genetics the study of elements constituting chromosomes, genes and cells is constantly revealing new information. We are told, for example, that if a single amino-acid is wrong out of the three to five hundred that make up a hemoglobin molecule of his blood, a man can die of sicklecell anemia.* In Chapter X we noted that man's hereditary characteristics are probably determined by the distribution of atoms within the genes, and if this is confirmed by later studies, intervention in the genetic build up of his body becomes a possibility. But on account of the billions of atoms contained in the trillions of cells of each individual this is still a very distant possibility. Which is all to the good because of the dangerous implications of such intervention before man acquires sufficient wisdom for directing individual and collective destinies. In the first place, we risk offsetting nature's natural selection. But even admitting that in time man might be able to replace in this field the element of chance by foresight, today we still shrink from genetic intervention being aware of past abuses in the name of racism as under Hitler, or similar kinds of fanaticism.

Education and Research

Education is the key to the future. In our technological age only the countries with the largest numbers of first class scientists and technicians can hope to maintain their status. In the ideological struggle with Communism, education plays a decisive role. Soviet Russia had in 1963 fifty-seven million people engaged in study, of whom seven million attended a university, against the United States' forty-five million of whom over four million are in universities or colleges.**

---

* Cf. Theodosius Dobzhansky in "Mankind Evolving".
** Figures of 1962. In the U.S. there will moreover be seven and a half million high school drop-outs, unless we improve our educational system.

Problems of the Future

Even more important is the fact that in the Age of Reason education becomes as indispensable to man as eating and drinking. Of all problems that face man, education and research will have the most immediate effect on his future. For they will help him to face the countless new challenges which the future has in store for him and to strengthen his capacity for foresight and thus to increase his control over his destiny. In order to train him for this, modern educators confront the student with concepts just beyond his grasp, sowing seeds in his subconscious, and at the same time stimulating his curiosity, creativity and ambition.

In the sphere of practical life, students can only acquire sufficient earning power if they gain a rudimentary knowledge of modern science, technology, automation, etc. Tomorrow's economy has fewer and fewer jobs for the ignorant. * Distinct efforts for reforms in American education are under way. Our federal government, which has to see to it that our educational effort does not lag behind that of other countries, has made large sums available to the states who, in turn, resolutely try to cope with the mounting demands for education and to improve the quality of teaching.

A new attitude towards education is noticeable in the American home. Instead of shielding their children from the outside world, or of personifying a cold and merciless society in order to make them pliable and prepared to conform, parents are becoming more inclined to encourage their children to fend for themselves and rely upon their own judgment. They portray the world as anything but hostile, rather as a living community in which the child will find his niche, be given his education and an opportunity to unfold his abilities and talents, and towards which he has duties and obligations. In primary education the trend is to make a child solve his problems independent of outside help, and this is extended to the entire learning period. Children are made to understand that their world of tomorrow will present different problems from those of today and that it is up to their generation to find the answers, and this develops a sense of

* Today in large cities such as Chicago there are still ten thousands of "ignorants", fifty per cent of whom are functional illiterates incapable of reading street names or simple instructions.

self-reliance, self-discipline and responsibility. Children are taught that all changes in the world result from an uninterrupted chain of thinking through the ages. Learning to project their own thinking into the future and then to look back helps them to detect the changing nature of values. This teaches them to think independently and to overcome superstition and prejudice. They are told that hatred is due to ignorance. The ignorance of how to use one's brain, which leads to copying others, conforming to the ideas of others, accepting slogans and, ultimately, falling prey to hysteria instead of exercising rational objectivity.

At a certain moment the question arises whether a student's education must be specialized or remain, at least partly, generalized. This is a timely and important problem. In a way it reflects the present ideological struggle. Functional specialization is mandatory in Communist countries in order to prevent the masses from falling prey to non-conformist ideas in philosophy and politics. Communist education is the opposite of generalized education. Its aim is not to make students into independent men and women but to forge them into cogs of the social machine. This kind of functional specialization opens the road to partial atrophy of the mind and goes against the trend of man's evolution.

The free world avoids this pitfall. It also goes in for specialization but only upon the foundation of a reasonably all-round knowledge. For students to embark on a specialized field without possessing such basic knowledge is considered tantamount to wilfully reducing the range of activity of their minds. The broader the foundation of general knowledge, the freer and more independent their thinking can become and the greater their ease in finding a synthesis between their own and other fields of knowledge. In some universities such different disciplines as history, political science, philosophy and social science are being interrelated and the tendency is to further extend this. The idea is even to combine physics, biology, and mathematics with the humanities. At first this may seem a hopeless endeavor but the intention is to facilitate it with the help of computers.

Today's business schools teach production, distribution, marketing, consumer research, accounting, etc. not as separate courses but as a single coordinated science accessible with the help of technological tools. Such institutes as Graduate Schools for Industrial Administration produce top scientific managers whose ready knowledge equals or surpasses that acquired through long experience by their older colleagues. Their thinking has been constantly focused on long range research and on planning and foresight.

In our American colleges and universities not only learning but also thinking has become the order of the day, students being told that independent thinking is more important than memorizing facts. Americans are breaking away from the old notion that science is an accumulation of factual knowledge and recognize research for what it is, a means for developing scientific theory with the help of creative imagination and visionary insight based on known facts. We are no longer surprised when the discovery of new facts upsets what we considered as axiomatic truths or if what we mistook for facts proved to be illusions requiring us to overhaul our thinking.

Gradually basic research turns to other than utilitarian or functional goals and follows the soaring imagination of the theoretical scientist. In our widening perspective knowledge of facts gives way to the more subtle art of arranging facts in an imaginary curve that provides a key for future inventions and discoveries and a basis for foresight. Thus theories are developed that literally open up new horizons. So vast has become the available knowledge in even a single branch of science, that teamwork and cooperation on the largest possible international scale has become a must in any kind of research. The ivory tower belongs to the past. Only in the heated atmosphere of discussion can man hope to keep abreast of evolution's relentless pressure.

Research makes man realise his potentialities and opens windows on the future. It thus protects him against those who prefer to close these windows and push him back in the stuffy room of the past because their own thinking does not go beyond its dimensions and because they believe that in this room they can get the better of him. Research is of decisive importance. Research is a new dynamic orientation of the world towards a new scale of values.

It is still mostly conducted in the exact sciences, * but the

---

* Federal expenditure for research amounted in 1962 to nearly fifteen billion dollars, of which 650 million was for medical research and only one million for research in the humanities.

breakthrough in evolution and biology foreshadows new research departures in the social sciences. In these fields new theories are turning up which may prove of greater importance to man than the latest discoveries in the world of physics.

A New Dimension in Thinking

In reviewing some of the problems which await us in the immediate future, we avoided hazarding ourselves in the sphere of pure science. But there is one kind of problem, currently considered as a test of contemporary man's thinking capacity, namely the concept of a time-space continuum, which deserves to be mentioned. It requires an effort to think of time as a dimension and the average man can only hope to approximate the meaning of such a "fourth" dimension. As an understanding of the time-space continuum is regarded as decisive for man's advance in thinking or, if one prefers, for man's next mutation of the mind, a few leads to the problem follow.

If we look at a star that is a thousand light years away, we do not see it as it is today but as it was a thousand years ago. In the same way an observer on a star five hundred light years away observing the earth with a super-telescope would not see us as we are, but would observe events as they took place during the Middle Ages, say the voyages of Columbus. So we understand that in space, time is linked up with distance. If we look at a person's pictures, taken when he was a child, a grown-up or in his old age, we obviously see three totally different three-dimensional representations of the same being who, however, remains the same and therefore must be four-dimensional. So we get an inkling of what the fourth dimension is.

Einstein taught that great velocities, such as produced in a cyclotron, make an iron rod shrink and a clock slow down. If the velocity reaches the speed of light the rod is reduced to nothing and the clock stops. So we understand that a man's heartbeat because the heart is a kind of clock can be slowed down at great speed and his other bodily functions similarly reduced to a minimum. Assuming that an astronaut in a space ship reaches 99% of the speed of light, logic tells us that at his homecoming from a trip to a star ten light

years away, his clock would show, and his bodily functions
confirm, that only three years had gone by. He would therefore be only three years older while people on earth would
have aged twenty years. So again we have to conclude that
distance and duration are interconnected. * The explanation
given is that the earth's gravity slows down gamma rays
that travel to its center. It follows that gamma rays, slowed
down by gravitational fields, disturb or equally slow down
the regular flow of energy, including the energy that maintains life, thus shortening the duration of the life span.
We conclude that to age results from gravitational influences
which, while slowing down gamma rays apparently speed
up clocks, the alternation of sun-rises and sun-sets, and
the succession of generations, speeding up the duration and
thus shortening the life span of each. And so we see that in
space, duration and time are influenced by the absence or
presence of gravitational fields, the next problem being to
analyse what these gravitational fields really are.

To make matters more difficult, the moment we penetrate
in the microcosmos, it becomes still harder to think in terms
of a time space continuum. How far we are from catching
more than a glimpse of what goes on in the microcosmos is
illustrated by our still imperfect knowledge of what goes on in
the atom. According to the latest experiments with an
electron accelerator only electrons seem to have a material
existence while protons and neutrons seem to have no core
at all and consequently occupy no space. We are therefore
at a loss to understand how these infinitesimal particles
behave in time and space. Our research amounts as yet to
little more than a number of disconnected discoveries permitting only tentative hypotheses that must be continuously
revised. This, more than anything else, induces us to look
at the future which will gradually divulge more, adding to
our small knowledge and diminishing our huge ignorance.
For man's thirst of knowledge is unquenchable.

---

* Cf. an article in "Life", June 17, 1963.

Chapter XIII

THE SCIENCE OF EVOLUTION
OFFERS A WAY OUT OF THE POLITICAL IMPASSE

It is time to return to our main theme which is how to overcome the present evolutionary crisis and to extricate the
world from the cold war. In our summary of the Theory of
Evolution a few concepts emerged which have a direct
bearing on our political problem and offer statesmen a basic
approach for overcoming the Cold War.

We found evolution to be an irreversible movement irresistibly carried forward by the very cosmic forces which put
it into motion. A movement that creates incredible diversity
and even greater complexity and refinement in the midst of
an all-pervasive unity. Evolution culminates in man, and man's
mind is the most highly perfected instrument which evolution
has produced to date. Reason has become man's basic virtue.
Reason demands independent thinking and thus freedom.

The interdependence of everything in the universe brings
home to man the oneness of mankind. The urge towards
association, which was a mechanism for the expansion of
life, influenced man in a particular way. During thousands of
years man lived in tribes and communities which had little
or no contact. During the last millennia mankind began to
converge and the center of gravity to shift from the individual
to the collectivity. Mankind began to develop into a single
living organism. A sphere of inter-thinking was born and
grew, and evolution entered a new phase. Under the influence
of the noosphere slow biological mutations changed into
mutations of the mind and man's progress was tremendously
accelerated.

This provides the basic arguments for the solution of our
political problem. We are now aware that man's continued
evolution requires:
(1) A further refining and perfecting of the individual's mind;
(2) Mankind's continued development into a single living
organism;

(3) Constant interaction between the individual mind and the collective brain as a means of stimulating the progress of both. We also know:

(1) That perfecting the individual's mind requires freedom, which is the basic tenet of the free world's philosophy;
(2) That mankind's totalization requires a collective effort which is a basic tenet of Communism, and
(3) That the interaction between individual mind and collective brain offers the key to a synthesis between the two opposed ideologies.

This provides a way out of the present explosive situation. The pieces of our puzzle begin to fall into place, and a number of questions that came up in our study find an answer. If freedom and collectivity no longer stand in insurmountable opposition, but are both indispensable to man's evolution, they are elements of a new synthesis, and the Cold War no longer has a "raison d'être". It will take time to translate this into practical politics, but the direction is there and the pattern is given.

However, switching from theory to practice, transforming the abstract long-view into a concrete short-view approach, raises a number of questions.

Which is the Right Approach?

The first question is what steps should be taken in order to get people at home and abroad in the free world, among the uncommitted nations, and among the Communists themselves to move in the direction indicated by science. Right away we encounter a dilemma. Must the effort be made with the help of an abstract vision or through a practical approach? The latter requires changing the conditions under which people live in order automatically to suggest new thoughts to them. If it is to be assumed that their natural inertia and conservatism is such that abstract reasoning has no effect on them, it is better to follow the practical approach. However, all through history masses were swayed by abstract ideas. Besides this, the practical approach misses this point: that to improve his mind, man must be helped to overcome his aversion to thinking, not through the routine of changed conditions, but through an effort of his own. This pleads for the theoretical approach.

A Way out of the Political Impasse

The Abstract Appeal

The use of abstractions in politics is as old as civilization. Liberty, equality, democracy, Fascism, Communism and others, as numerous and varied as imagination or opportunism require, achieved their political purpose, provided that they had the right appeal to the people's emotion. Consequently the abstract concepts postulated by the theory of evolution should be expressed in terms so simple and moving as to produce a genuine emotional reaction. This is necessary because every fresh departure from past traditions produces the impulse to reject what is new in the everlasting struggle between the spirit that denies and the spirit that creates. In the present stage of his development chances are that man is able to understand that Communism pursues the totalisation * of mankind under its banner at the expense of individual liberty, and the West, freedom of the individual at the expense of mankind's solidarity, and that both ideologies fail to recognize the unbreakable tie which exists between freedom and the oneness of the human race, both of which are essential to man's further advance. If an adjustment of the basic tenets of the free and Communist ideologies seems at present difficult of attainment, the theory of evolution is at least likely to be accepted as providing a higher level of thinking out of which a synthesis between both ideologies may eventually be derived.

Statesmen ready to invoke conclusions based on the theory of evolution must possess a scientific turn of mind as well as moral elevation. In order to make the necessary spiritual impact, their message must inspire man all over the world:

(1) to regard his destiny, or rather the destiny of the human race, as of greater interest than anything else, encouraging him to probe the secrets of nature and of the universe and never to relent;

(2) to march together with others in order to explore the immense fields of future knowledge that at present are still beyond his ken;

---

* Totalisation not in the political sense of bringing under totalitarian rule, but in the philosophical sense of compressing into a single organism.

157

A Way out of the Political Impasse

(3) to find in every advance, in every discovery, in every invention a further incentive to perfect his thinking and that of the community of men;

(4) to realise in the throes of ever mounting tensions that his and mankind's survival depend on mutual understanding and help and on a change from traditional enmity to sympathy, for only thus can he aspire to the extraordinary destiny which science forecasts for the human race;

(5) to unite with others in order to reach the point where he can overcome the laws of chance that rule the material world and, with the help of foresight, influence his and mankind's destiny;

(6) to turn away from all that keeps him back or thwarts his efforts, so that his preoccupations with profit, power and other material designs will fade in comparison with the adventures his mind can conjure, with the result that problems of daily subsistence will become as automatic as the registration of an image by the eye, freeing his mind for ever more complicated tasks; finally

(7) to open his heart and seek others in love.

Statesmen know that the practical application of such a vision requires a long and patient effort, but in the meantime it can help to dissipate prevailing uncertainties and frustrations. It offers a new incentive able to generate energy and to bring a zest for living, and also a glimpse of immortality. It offers man a new purpose, philosophically, morally and politically.

Philosophically, it demands from man the understanding that evolution not only leads to unification of the human race but also to a convergence of minds and common mental efforts. According to Julian Huxley it is "the long-range task of the human species" to achieve this "fully conscious common purpose of convergence of the minds" with the help of a "common pool of knowledge and experience".

Morally, the new purpose requires that man, endowed with a mind which nature continually further refines, recognizes the obligation to think independently as a prerequisite for assuming responsibility towards himself and towards others. Thus the ancient precepts of "know thyself" and "love thy neighbor" become evolutionary demands, and the age-old search for the right relationship between individual and society reaches global dimensions.

158

A Way out of the Political Impasse

Politically, the new purpose aims at the unification of mankind without sacrificing man's personality. * For the first time man perceives a pattern in his evolutionary advance between the drive for individual freedom and the totalisation of mankind. In the past he was convinced that man's future lay in the direction either of freedom or of collectivity. Hence his failure to see that behind the façade of the Cold War lies a far deeper crisis — a crisis which springs from man's inability to recognize the nature of his evolution and to understand that far from having to lead to a holocaust, the tension between freedom and collectivity is vital to his future.

The Practical Approach

However this may be, the practical approach must also be followed. Several modern sociologists believe that only through changed circumstances can people be induced to change their thinking. Jean Monnet once said that Frenchmen, Germans, Dutchmen, etc. will only begin to think of a united Europe after the conclusion of a European customs union, the introduction of a European currency, a European legislation encouraging the migration of labor without loss of national social advantages, etc. Practical steps for making people conscious of the new approach suggested by the theory of evolution must consist of promoting every conceivable form of international cooperation, more particularly between free and Communist nations. Cooperation, for example, in scientific and technological research, space or deep-sea exploration, and all sorts of global operations or assistance which reveal mankind as a living entity to the average man and help to sublimate artificial barriers between nations.

Every presentation of war as a crime against humanity, of poverty as a global rather than national evil, of disease as a world-wide and not local affliction, and fear as a paralysis that grips mankind rather than any specific nation or individual, gives to the concept of mankind a living reality. Nothing unites men more than common misfortune, difficulties or fear, and nothing is more apt to make them cooperate. Keeping

---

* Personality in the sense of realization of man's inner self as distinct from individuality which merely distinguishes between the single and the multiple.

159

faith with the United Nations, notwithstanding its present relative weakness, highlights the fact that the world has embarked upon a period of growing interdependence from which
there is no return. Any assistance to underdeveloped countries
underlines the fact that responsibility of the great and prosperous powers for smaller and less fortunate ones has become
axiomatic, and that isolation of the past is being replaced by
solidarity. In our cooperative dealings with the Communist
world the accent should be put on the individual, making it
clear that every contribution of each of the participants in
international cooperation is essential to further progress,
and that the creative capacity of the individual is what sets
collective thought processes and global efforts going.

Power still Prevails

Before any abstract or practical approach can be undertaken
with a hope of success, the prevailing climate in international
relations must change. For at the moment power is still the
decisive element in the world. True, many a statesman is
convinced that common sense will ultimately predominate and
that a cataclysm will be avoided by replacing the rule of force
by the rule of law, but the tangible reality of today is that power
still prevails. In view of the acceleration of man's thinking
processes there is hope that this will gradually make way for a
more enlightened attitude. In the meantime, power politics
share the fate of all institutions which, on their way to disappear, seem to yield a maximum of energy in their final
convulsions.

To the diplomat and soldier responsible for his country's
security, the balance of power continues to constitute the
decisive element in international politics. Power, and its
companion prestige, go on to play a considerable role in
diplomacy. But since nuclear war has become suicidal and
since conventional wars risk escalating into nuclear war,
power and prestige considerations are less likely to lead to
armed conflicts than in the past.

Nevertheless, power as concentrated in the United States,
the Soviet Union and other leading nations represents an
important part of the accumulated energy of mankind. Such
formidable forces cannot forever be contained. Unless
channeled into creative outlets, they risk unleashing their

160

pent-up energy in violence. Great nations are having a second look at the nature of power and are groping for means to consult with one another to overcome the present world crisis without too great a loss of prestige and too much sacrifice of national pride. This can best be achieved by a <u>combined</u> attack of all nations on the global problems that besiege humanity. To this end the best brains will have to embark on a world-wide cooperation.

The reader may properly remark that if the ideological tension can be removed, other tensions will come up because tensions are the source of the energy without which there can be no progress. The very nature of evolution lies in the self-propelling movement caused by the interplay of opposed forces. Tension will remain as long as there is the one and the multiple, but it will assume a number of different aspects. The question is whether these new tensions will pose a new threat of war. Since war became a losing proposition in the nuclear age, the kind of religious or prestige wars of the past are unlikely to occur again. The same goes for ideological wars, provided there is a strong enough deterrent. Lesser wars for territorial aggrandizement are likely to encounter such world-wide criticism as to give the United Nations the necessary authority to prevent them. There remain wars for the defense of vital interests threatened by a sudden disruption of the existing power equilibrium. Cuba was an indication that even under such circumstances war can be avoided provided that any such danger is met with speed and determination. The same may apply to what the Communist call wars of "liberation", which are really armed Communist interventions to make a Communist inspired revolution succeed. If the free world moves fast enough to prevent any miscalculation, the Communists are likely to desist. The main danger to peace lies today in what might be called wars of desperation. Wars of the have-nots, whose misery is such that even war seems preferable to the continuation of unbearable conditions.

If the have-nots in all countries of the southern hemisphere were one day to unite against the more prosperous haves of the northern hemisphere, a new split could arise in the world, a split at which Red China is apparently aiming. The tension between East and West would then be replaced by a South-North tension, but if such a re-alignment is recognized in time, the necessary preventive measures can be devised to combat poverty, which is its main motivation.

At present, with the Cold War still going on and the power struggle still dominating the international scene, every statesman is faced with the problem of how to help mankind obtain a deeper understanding—which we called the long view—before the irreparable happens. This requires daily efforts to keep things moving, to avoid explosions and to inculcate a new mentality all over the world. What this implies in the conduct of American foreign policy, in the first place towards Communism, is tentatively suggested in the next chapters.

Chapter XIV

AMERICAN FOREIGN POLICY

The Need for a Positive Policy

In order to devise a foreign policy it is necessary to discern and analyse the titanic forces of history to which mankind is exposed and which are nothing less than the forces of evolution. The scientific effort required for this, matches in importance any plan of direct action. Both are necessary and it is from their combined application that a foreign policy is born and a nation's destiny forged.

There is quite a time lag between the elaboration of a foreign policy plan and the achievement of concrete results. All that the search for a basic policy can momentarily produce is a state of mind with which to tackle political problems. It is impossible to guess how long it will take before this shows results. It is equally impossible to achieve any lasting solutions through any other method. Here lies the art and the difficulty, the art of exercising foresight by means of the long view, and the difficulty of transforming the long view into concrete actions. Here also lies the difference between European and American diplomacy. European governments work out their diplomacy on the basis of carefully conceived plans and abstract principles, while we prefer to tackle our foreign problems from case to case with the help of a dash of commonsense. It is this attitude of ours which makes us think that our President simply has to choose from a number of concrete decisions for every problem that arises instead of visualizing him as a man—such as President Kennedy undoubtedly was—who not only tries to foresee coming events but works out in his mind a system of basic principles by which he can influence their course.

Generally speaking, Washington has a sharply partitioned number of foreign policies, for enemies and for friends, with this in common: it often veers from an endeavor to obtain long-range objectives to a perhaps more satisfactory

163

but, in terms of national interests, less rewarding search for popularity. What in private life is an admirable quality, the desire to please, is out of place in foreign policy. In power politics no attitude is taken at face value but is always meant to cause a reaction. In such a world, search for popularity stands in no connection to leadership and denotes either weakness or hypocrisy. Hence this policy usually achieves the opposite of what it aims at. Anti-Americanism is on the increase all over the world. Not only in countries which seek a scapegoat for their failures or a butt for their insecurity, but even among our allies. In Europe anti-Americanism is moreover mixed up with our much criticized lack of abstract thinking, a field in which Europeans pride themselves on their superiority.

If we could add to the coordination of power, determination and decisiveness which President Kennedy showed in the Cuba affair—and which stirred our allies—the gift of forethought, this would earn the United States the respect of the world, which is more important than their applause. It is this combination of forethought and dynamic action which may be decisive for our leadership. If we want to lead, as we must, it is not enough to react to circumstances, whether they are Communist acts of aggression or unexpected new initiatives of our allies or others, but we have to set ourselves, and possibly others, long-term goals.

It has been said that the world in its present profound transformation resulting from the scientific breakthrough —or as we should rather say from the new stage reached by man's evolution—is becoming allergic to leadership. This is not so. Leadership is as necessary to man as education, it all depends on the kind of leadership. It stands to reason that the leadership of yesterday is rejected today. American leadership based on political hegemony or on the achievements of the American people, and thus on the American way of life, is no longer acceptable. What is acceptable, even sought after, is American leadership based on a sense of global responsibility and service to others, the kind of service we render, not always adequately, with our foreign aid and successfully with our Peace Corps.

It is probably this kind of leadership which the American people had in mind when it elected President Kennedy. His election by a bare majority gave him no mandate. His "new

164

frontier" approach did not voice a popular demand but was an act of leadership and its general endorsement proved that a new departure was indeed what the people wanted. If in the United States a President succeeded in convincing a large majority of the need of a policy of global understanding, there is no reason why such a vision cannot inspire the whole of mankind. This became obvious after Kennedy's death. It was as if the shock of his assassination gave people all over the world a flash of intuition into mankind's destiny. At that moment nations felt linked by invisible ties. World leaders gathered together in Washington and it was as if an understanding for the oneness of mankind rose from the subconscious and illuminated the hearts of men and nations in their grief over a lost leader.

How to Work out a Foreign Policy

One of the difficulties in working out the details of a coherent foreign policy is that so many scholars and experts are called upon to advise the government. The analysis of alternative possibilities with their endless numbers of variations has the effect of splintering the efforts and of making the State Department lose sight of the main line of policy. Yet a definite policy with a single, coordinated pursuit is needed. It is not always the procedure we follow. The remarkable result of these many consultations is that they are used as a substitute for thinking through the entire complex of foreign policy and making overall decisions.

Too often our approach to foreign policy follows the military example, which is to work out to the smallest detail a number of eventualities. But the military have "a priori" to reckon with war, while in the international field the art is to avoid war. It would moreover be futile to envisage a decade in the seventies in which the armament race has doubled the amount of lethal weapons, or to study the contingencies of a preventive war, because the present trend is unquestionably away from war, and failure to prevent nuclear war would under the circumstances mean total failure of our foreign policy. It would be a waste of time to prepare for a world of autarchic nations or blocs surrounded by high tariff walls, because the aim of foreign policy is not to wait and then react to the designs of others, but to set oneself a goal in accordance to one's best understanding, which in this case is to raise the standards of living everywhere by the liberalization of world trade. It would be equally inept to make plans for a decade of armed containment of Communism in view of the fact that the Cold War is already losing its impetus and that long since we have recognized that in the last analysis it cannot be overcome by force of arms but by a change of mind. All such studies risk falling into the same error of starting from a given situation and then assuming that conditions remain as they are, whereas in reality they continuously change.

The foremost problem of American foreign policy is to define the United States' long-term objectives, and not to determine how to react to the policies of others. The second problem is how the United States is to reconcile its policy with contrary designs of others. Finally, how it is going to manoeuvre in order to guide the world in what it has come to regard as the right direction.

The first objective is to end the Cold War and transform a climate of ideological tension into one of cooperation between the free and Communist worlds. Collaboration in a number of practical and scientific fields will lessen suspicion and bring about a beginning of understanding. In this policy no direct reference should be made to the ideological differences, but an effort made to approach them from an entirely new angle, namely that of the demands of evolution. The tool to be used is creative imagination. With its help other trends can be initiated:

(1) Promotion of a trend away from nationalism and toward regional or continental integration whether in Europe, Latin America, Africa, Asia, or towards the integration of a still larger entity, the Atlantic Community, in order to strengthen the ties of freedom;

(2) Support and aid to these groupings on a regional rather than national basis, especially in Europe and Latin America;

(3) Efforts to safeguard peace and order among the new nations in Africa and Asia in order to give them time to organize their administration before seeking added security in regional federations;

(4) Continued rationalization of international conflicts, bringing to bear all our influence and authority whether alone, with others, or through the United Nations;

(5) Support of the United Nations and of the use of its

Emergency Force as the forerunner of a regular International Police Force;

(6) Promotion of international disarmament;

(7) World-wide war on poverty, disease and inadequate education, etc.

A new approach might be sought in the Far East by a shift from military to economic, social and educational assistance, leading up to a recognition of Red China, affording not only Moscow but also Peking an escape hatch to the West and a rapprochement with the free world that could bring about a revision of the aims of Communism.

The foresight to establish new trends rests on a correct analysis of past events and their complicated entanglements that can only be discerned by hindsight. A single example can explain this. One of the contributary reasons for Khrushchev's hurried retreat in Cuba may have been his foreknowledge of China's impending attack on India. Had the Kremlin persisted in its Cuba venture, the entire world would have been convinced that the Communists had set up a double-pronged attack against the free world. Russia would have been carried along in Peking's war policy and unable to revert to co-existence. This caused the Kremlin to disassociate itself from Peking and, after some hesitation, to abandon its intention of seeking to redress the American superiority in ICBM's by withdrawing its short-range missiles from Cuba, and to deliver the promised MIG planes to Nehru. Seen by Chinese eyes this intricate affair has still another side. It is possible that Peking, aware of Khrushchev's plan to build a missile base in Cuba, timed its war against India in order to make it coincide with Russia's hazardous Cuban coup which, it hoped, would prevent Russia from helping India. China's subsequent cease-fire offer became inevitable when Soviet Russia saw through the manoeuvre, removed its missiles from Cuba and stuck to its promise to send fighter planes to India. Faced with American and Russian opposition, Peking had to give in.

Revision of Treaties

An important matter in the field of foreign policy is the revision of treaties. Treaties tend to become obsolete and obligations assumed at a certain time to become an inequitable burden under changed circumstances. Countless efforts made by the League of Nations and the United Nations to find a solution to this problem failed. It is therefore up to the parties concerned to seek a reasonable adjustment of outdated treaties. And it is up to the more powerful of the parties to take the initiative in proposing a revision. The United States could have spared itself a great deal of unpleasantness, if it had voluntarily and spontaneously adjusted some of the treaties concluded during the Theodor Roosevelt's "big stick" period of diplomacy. Treaties like those concluded with Panama in 1903 about the Canal and with Cuba in the same year about the Guantanamo base are bound, after sixty years, to arouse discontent. If a nation as powerful as the United States spontaneously proposes the revision of outdated treaties, this increases its stature and prestige in the world and, moreover, promotes goodwill among the treaty partners and sometimes even produces a "quid-pro-quo". This is preferable to having to yield under adverse public opinion, reluctantly give up one's rights and be insulted to boot.

Congress and Foreign Policy

Should the Department of State decide that certain definite lines of foreign policy are in the interest of the U.S. and of the world at large, the President and the Secretary of State need freedom of movement and less interference by Congress than in the past. It is the President's responsibility to frame a foreign policy, while it is Congress' task to ratify or reject treaties concluded by the executive, and to express general views on foreign politics, but not to interfere with detailed operations which in their totality lead up to an American foreign policy. If a public opinion develops which opposes a trend in our foreign policy, if for example the view prevails in certain states of our Union that closer contact with the Communists might be dangerous and useless, senators up for re-election might feel inclined to oppose such a rapprochement. However, no foreign policy should be impeded by electoral preoccupations, for it must be judged on its overall merits either by acceptance or rejection of treaties which are milestones in a general policy, or by popular approval or disapproval in presidential elections.

168

Adaptation of Foreign Policy

President Johnson once said that the U.S. has as many foreign policies as there are countries in the world. By this he obviously meant that there should be a variety of adaptations of our basic policy to various countries. For in the age of reason we must have a single rational line of policy. Even if it does not yet occur to the majority of the people, or to a number of politicians, officials and newsmen to look for a motivation above the level of the present inconclusive ideological strife, recent scientific conclusions can play a decisive role and be given a fair try in determining our foreign policy. For it has to guide us through nothing less than the decisive fight for men's minds and for their very existence.

As to a countrywide adaptation of our foreign policy, a few suggestions are presented in the final chapters. Beginning with our relations with underdeveloped countries, with Latin America, Japan, our European allies, Red China, the Satellites and Cuba, it leads up to the crux of the matter which is the U.S. - U.S.S.R. relationship.

Chapter XV

AMERICAN FOREIGN ECONOMIC AND MILITARY AID

The U.S. and the Underdeveloped Countries

The concept of foreign aid arose after the war. Truman's Point IV Program and the Marshall Plan aimed at putting Western Europe again on its feet. Partly dictated by national self-interest and partly as a manifestation of selflessness, U.S. aid was later extended to other countries as the means of discharging some of its obligations of world leadership. Soon the American example was followed by other Western countries, when they became more consciously aware of the interdependence of all nations.

The principle of foreign aid is not unanimously supported in the U.S. Its opponents are of the opinion that such expenditures as might unbalance the budget and endanger the stability of the dollar, and incidentally of their personal capital, are contrary to the United States' interests. They apparently still live under the illusion of an island of American prosperity in a sea of poverty, and do not understand that unless opportunities are created for the have-nots in the only way that is presently feasible, namely through foreign aid, the resulting world-wide misery will finally undermine their own prosperity. The criticism that U.S. aid does not always get into the right pockets, and that some of the aid plans result from prestige demands of the recipients rather than from economic needs, are not altogether unfounded. It is, therefore quite an achievement that successive administrations have succeeded in overcoming the combined opposition of Democratic and Republican conservatives against what they called sacrificing direct American interests for the sake of a future and nebulous world order. But there are no two ways about it: if the U.S. is prepared to assume responsibility for other nations, foreign aid cannot be rejected as squandering the nation's resources. It is a means of obviating the kind of poverty and distress that breeds subversion, and at the same time a recognition of the unity of mankind and of a duty which transcends American short-time interests. This, however, does not imply that American democracy and the American way of life should be held up to the recipients and exalted to the point of requiring them to follow it.

Russia and China's contributions to foreign aid are only fractions of the assistance provided by the U.S. and its Western allies. From 1955 to mid 1962 the U.S. spent 24.4 billion dollars in foreign help and the Soviet Union committed 4.9 billion dollars, of which 1.2 billion had been drawn by June 30, 1962. Communist aid is motivated by considerations of power and propaganda as, for example, Russia's considerable contribution to Indonesian armament to protect that country from Peking's imperialism. American foreign help also has political connotations, but apart from that it shows a genuinely disinterested concern for others. To a lesser degree the Communist aid also serves that aim, and therefore the difference in amounts spent by the free and Communist worlds is not overly important. What matters is that both antagonists introduced into a traditionally ego-centric foreign policy an element of responsibility for others. This can eventually offer a basis for cooperation between them.

In giving aid to the newly independent countries we have to distinguish clearly between our objectives and theirs. If we hope that our assistance will stimulate their desire for freedom, we have to bear in mind that their ideas about freedom are still vague. As long as it meant escape from colonialism it had appeal. To countries hungry for the long denied riches of their former colonial rulers, freedom loses much of its attraction. Our contention that only in a free and competitive society can a maximum of efficiency be achieved, passes their understanding. Their views are still ensconced in a world of material rewards. They point out that the Communists also say that their system is based on freedom and that their particular mixture of "freedom" and discipline enabled them to achieve fast and spectacular results. For countries whose overriding desire is to reach the age of industrialization and modernization as quickly as possible, the Communist example is indeed attractive. To them our insistence on political freedom seems academic and less important than catching up with the rest of the world in technical skills, productivity and living standards. Our contention that political freedom creates

171

the best guarantee against tyranny in whatever form, is lost on people who consider indigenous tyranny as an evil to be accepted in the bargain for achieving immediate results. As a matter of fact, only five out of the more than thirty-five new African states practice parliamentary democracy, all others having adopted an authoritarian, or having reverted to a more rudimentary, form of government.

Every modern economy - and the newly independent countries have firmly decided to create a new and dynamic economy - faces the problem of how to create an adequate industrial apparatus. The first to solve it was Western Europe, then came the U.S. and finally the Soviet Union in the nineteen-twenties. Today it confronts all countries which recovered their·national independence, such as India, Pakistan, China, Indonesia, the Congo and all the other new African and Asian states. To all those who are used to magnifying the differences between capitalist and Communist economies, it may seem strange that there is but one single method to achieve this aim. No modern industry can be built without withholding from the workers during a period of time an important part of the fruits of their labor. In Europe the remainder went partly to the capitalists - what Marx called their exploitation of the working classes - but mostly it went into national industrial equipment. In Communist countries the greater part also goes into industrial equipment and the rest increases the finances of the state. Communist leaders call this the inevitable sacrifice before the millennium sets in. To the peoples of the new countries who hoped that independence from the white man would automatically provide them with his wealth, such a period of hard work without immediate and tangible results appears as an injustice. And if their governments receive aid from the West, they feel that this is to make up for this presumed injustice.

After the new countries shook off the white man's tutelage they fenced for a while for themselves. The multilateral relationship which they maintained with other nations via the mother country, changed to a unilateral contact with the outside world. It was for them like the experience of a young man who, on leaving college, faces the cold and merciless world. He is alternatively self-confident to the point of truculence of inclined to seek protection by joining one or the other group. Their choice at first followed the line of ideological demarcation. It did not last long before they tried their hand at playing both ends against the middle. But when certain ulterior motives of the Communist aid became apparent, it was time to reconsider.

It now looks as if the newly independent countries will increasingly turn to the West and to nationals of their former motherlands for advice in matters of commerce, industry and administration. How soon depends on the attitude of the Western powers themselves. The spontaneous way in which Britain ended its colonial rule in India permitted a more or less uninterrupted relationship with the motherland. France's enlightened attitude towards most of its African colonies resulted in a continued presence of French advisers in these countries. Belgium's readiness to give the Congo its independence, followed by a massive exodus of Belgians, facilitated soon afterwards their return in large numbers. On the other hand, France's uncompromising stand towards Algiers severed all relations with the new government until a recent visit of President Ben Bella to President de Gaulle. The same applies to the Dutch, whose return as advisers, businessmen and technicians to Indonesia only could begin after the New Guinea problem had been settled. Such normalization of relations with the West is likely to put an end to anti-Western hate campaigns and turn the new countries away from the ideological struggle in order to concentrate on revamping their economy which badly suffers from lack of adequately trained personnel. Here American aid can appear to full advantage. It will be welcome because the U.S. showed tact and understanding. This applies especially to the Peace Corps, whose aid went straight to the peoples' hearts. The Peace Corps was a master stroke because the help it provides is simple, given without any thought of ideological indoctrination and also because it puts into practice the typical American habit of community activities on the local level. Altogether this kind of aid awakens a sense of interdependence and security.

As, notwithstanding foreign aid, poverty is still deepening in many of the neediest countries, the distribution of food to the hungriest nations becomes an acute problem. The United States, Canada and Australia can achieve a great deal by dumping surplus food below cost price in these countries, thereby saving high storage costs. There is no cheaper method for combating disorder and Communism. And if this should be frowned upon by other food exporting countries, the question must be thrashed out in a world conference in line with other efforts to arrive at a gradual world-wide redistribution of purchasing power.

If the present détente between the United States and Soviet Union continues, the ensuing cooperation may extend to the field of foreign aid. The above-mentioned disparity between American and Soviet aid might militate against it. On the other hand, help given in common removes the element of ideological competition and permits the aid program to be, at least in part, operated through the United Nations, a means of strengthening this organization.

This implies the participation of other countries in foreign aid. Not only of our Western allies but of all white countries. For of the world's 123 countries, of which 90 with a population of 2 billion are poor, the remaining 33 with one billion people are rich and, coincidentally, are all white. For the first time the latter have become aware of impending events which cast a long shadow ahead. The shadow of a widening rift and desperate clash because the existing gap between the living standards and trade of the haves and have-nots increases year by year. From 1950 to 1960 exports of the have-nots dropped by 26%, and their share in world trade from 30% to 20%, while the West's share increased from 60% to 66% and that of the Communist countries from 8% to 12%. The reason of this increasing disparity is that prices of raw materials which the poor nations must sell in order to be able to buy capital goods from the industrial countries sometimes fall, sometimes vary a little but never keep step with the continuous rise in prices of Western industrial goods and machinery.

This gap has to be bridged. And it must be bridged now. In this time of ours, in which the white man has reached the apogee of his power, he has become conscious of his global responsibilities. He knows that in the one world that must result from an ever more converging humanity, the present differences in living standards, or rather the present extremes between wealth and poverty, no longer can be maintained. Help must be given on a larger scale than hitherto, in different ways, and by more nations than at present.

Help must be larger because the deepening rift in trade and living standards must be halted. Assistance must be

different because incidental hand-outs, though at first in-
dispensible, must be replaced by a concerted effort of all
white nations. And more nations must contribute because
should things be permitted to drift, the existing gap will
become unbridgeable. It is therefore wise for the haves to
give liberally now in order to safeguard the remainder of
their accumulated capital. The problem is difficult and
requires a good deal of imagination. The old recipe of letting
private investment take care of it can no longer be applied.
Few of the poor countries are able to offer the guarantees
demanded by private investors in spite of pious admonitions
of harder work and more frugality. * However, a beginning
has been made by bringing the problem in the open. In the
spring of 1964 a U.N. Conference on Trade and Development
was opened in Geneva. Of the two thousand delegates from
the 121 participating countries, the majority, belonging to the
poor countries, hailed the conference as a constructive effort
undertaken by a U.N. on which they pin their faith as to their
future development. This conference cuts through the exclusi-
vity of the GATT negotiations. The General Agreement on
Trade and Tariffs was of old an instrument of bargaining
between competitive industrial nations, offering no leeway to
the non-industrialized have-nots with their scant bargaining
power.

It is too early at the time of writing to foresee the results
of the conference. A number of approaches have been suggested. One is to guarantee prices and steady sales of raw
materials by means of quota agreements as under the World
Sugar Agreement. This prevents sudden drops in prices,
cornering of commodities, and can even be used to raise
commodity prices. Another is to raise a tax on imports from
poor countries and use the amounts thus collected as a fund to
finance the poor countries' development programs, or to
raise their wage level in order to increase their purchasing
power. Still another is to discriminate in favor of underdeveloped countries by letting in their manufactured or semi-
manufactured goods duty free into the developed countries,
while maintaining tariffs against others. The old slogan of
"free access to raw materials for all" is replaced by that of

---

* The part of all capital investments destined to underdeveloped countries dropped from 43% in 1956 to 29% in 1964.

175

"adequate retribution to all producers of raw materials". In this way one of the most serious causes for succeeding economic world crises, namely the discrepancy between industrial and farm wages might ultimately be reduced.

Theoretically there is still another solution. If one per cent of the 120 billion dollars spent yearly on armaments by East and West went to the poor countries, they would find their resources tripled overnight. This would not only help to prevent the gap between haves and have-nots from further widening but could considerably reduce it. And, what is more interesting, this solution no longer seems unattainable. But this is not yet generally recognized, for there is already a good deal of opposition to the less radical proposals. Those countries among the haves, such as Britain, which must import nearly all their raw materials, balk at the extra burden which a levy would impose on them. However, such compensation could be made on a flexible scale taking into account both the amount of raw materials imported and the degree of unavailability of such materials in the importing country.

The U.S., though usually conservative in matters of trade, has always championed the cause of the underdeveloped countries. As against the conservative opposition against foreign aid, there is a growing understanding of a new approach in the U.S. which would let poor nations have the benefit at or below cost price of our eventual surplus production resulting from automation, and which would find means to increase their purchasing power through direct contributions of all well-to-do countries. The problem is not taxing to our intelligence so much as it is disturbing to our equanimity. We realise that soon we will have to radically change some of our ingrained trading habits.

It requires quite an effort of imagination to create the kind of world that corresponds to the demands of our time. Since man's gift of foresight has increased of late, his responsibility is augmented in the same ratio. We are startled by the fact that we no longer can put up with the misery of two thirds of mankind. The oneness of humanity is no longer a theoretical postulate, it has become a living reality. Because the existing disparity can only be remedied through a world-wide cooperation of all the haves, the Russians included, this in itself is sufficient to put an end to the present ideological strife.

176

The U.S. and the Organization of American States

The U.S. relationship with Latin America is delicate. Proud and touchy about their independence, the countries of Latin-America on the one hand seek protection and neighborly aid and on the other hand resent even a semblance of interference in their internal affairs. In the Alliance for Progress, Washington took this to heart, though perhaps not sufficiently. For it made U.S. assistance dependent on certain economic and social reforms. To become eligible for aid recipients are required (1) to spread the tax burden more equitably among various groups of population and raise its overall level, (2) to establish a central planning agency which works out five and ten year plans, and (3) to introduce agrarian reforms by redistribution of land and a change in the tenure system. Though reasonable in principle, it may raise difficulties in practice on account of Latin-American susceptibilities. And as U.S. foreign policy aims at results, it is better to go after results than after theory. If our neighbors are touchy about our demand for reforms as the price for our aid, we had better try and help them in a different way. This could be done by raising the world price for Latin-American raw materials, and by supplying them with industrial products at a price they can afford, and shifting the aid problem from the level of national to that of world economy.* To increase Latin-American purchasing power as a whole may be a better means to finally overcome their poverty than the country by country approach of the Alliance for Progress. Elimination of poverty is of greater help to any country than all other social reforms.

The same kind of flexibility is called for in protecting our neighbors against Castro's Communism. If they feel that they can look after themselves and, moreover, do not view the Cuban threat with the same concern as the U.S., we had better desist. Just as we incline today towards overcoming Soviet Communism without fighting it, they prefer to get the better of Castro without too much fanfare.

Time and again the U.S. is used as a scapegoat in internal Latin-American disturbances as, for instance, in Argentina when President Frondizi accepted in 1962 a 400 million dollar

---

*For an explanation see under "Automation" in Chapter XII, page 140.

loan and agreed to important private U.S. investments. His simultaneous decision to implement an O.A.S. agreement to sever relations with Castro raised a storm of protests about his subservience to "Yankee" capitalism. Anti-Americanism is the easiest rallying call for parties with the most divergent political views. But the U.S. cannot possibly set that right by increasing its help. This was exemplified in Brazil. In the beginning of 1964 its economy was threatened by a runaway inflation - notwithstanding its wealth in natural resources of iron ore, manganese, timber, gold, diamonds, coffee, etc. - and radical elements continued to press for abnormally high wages. Its civil service salaries absorbed 40% of the government budget as against 14% in the U.S. Then Washington left them to their own devices and temporarily suspended its foreign aid. Ultimately Brazil was able to rid itself of this menace, which shows that it is indeed more appropriate to suspend our aid to a country which mismanages its affairs than to insist on the fulfilment of certain conditions. However, it cannot be expected that the replacement of a President with leftist tendencies by a moderate can solve everything without more ado. In this connection it seems advisable to observe restraint in our appreciation of Latin-American "coups d'état", and to desist from too hasty congratulations and formal recognitions which are not commensurate with the reserve and dignity of a leading power.

In Latin-America the methods of the Peace Corps and the new approach by A.I.D., which often operates with the assistance of independent American university professors advising Latin-American governments, create a new spirit of international cooperation. U.S. commonsense and efficiency combined with Latin-American finesse form a particularly adequate mixture for finding the right approach to such global problems as equalization of living standards and the fostering of a regional spirit.

The U.S. and Japan

In our relationship with Japan, too, global considerations should have primacy over all others. This does not mean that we should not heed Japan's specific problems or its special mentality. However lucid and cogent the solutions we propose in coordinating our mutual interests may be in our own eyes, they have to be acceptable to our Japanese ally to produce a basis for the future.

The Japanese are a proud and temperamental people with a mentality different from ours. This became evident in 1960 when the minority party prevented passage of the Mutual Security Treaty with the U.S. by the simple expedient of walking out of parliament. Japan, though a democracy, does not always feel bound by majority decisions. To them politics is a matter of compromise. Should a majority party desire to bring a treaty before parliament, it has, in their view, first to come to terms with the minority parties behind closed doors. Another basic Japanese trait, which they have in common with other Orientals, is their concern for face. Having lost face in their long drawn-out war against China that began in 1937 and lasted till 1945, because the latter was the military weaker, they had to take on a more powerful opponent in order to regain face. That was one of the contributory factors of Japan's war against the U.S., for even a defeat by America would mitigate the loses of face in the China war.

General MacArthur's post-war policy in Japan was a feat of exemplary diplomacy which laid the basis for today's friendship between the two countries. But Japan wants to forge its own destiny and to keep out of the Cold War. Neither do the Japanese have much inclination towards neutrality, but with part of the businessmen eyeing the Red Chinese market as a natural outlet, and another part of the population seeking American protection against Communist expansion, Japan tends towards a position of non-involvement. So Japan's future course is uncertain and this reflects on the U.S. position in the Far East, which is based on the Japanese alliance.

There is no pat solution to this impasse. Time must run its course. It will take Red China much longer than Soviet Russia to rationalize the world situation. Meanwhile all Washington can do is to provide Japan with adequate markets in order to guarantee an acceptable living standard for its teeming masses. Besides that, the U.S. must maintain its position of strength, and the more we refrain from pressing the Japanese to continue the mutual security pact, the more likely they are to do this of their own accord.

In the past the Japanese believed in the Kwodo or "imperial

road" which indicated the right and honorable way to serve. Since this philosophy was misused for ultra-nationalistic purposes, it became discredited. If we could awaken Japanese interest in the philosophy of evolution with its indication of how to serve not one nation but all of mankind, this would enhance our position and raise American-Japanese friendship and cooperation to a new level. Were we to find in the Japanese mind a response to this concept, we would have the support of a proud and independent people in our efforts to overcome the present crisis in man's evolution.

Chapter XVI

THE U.S. AND THE ALLIES

Europe

At the end of World War II the nations of Europe found themselves surrounded by two super-powers of continental dimensions. These could, in the thinking of those days, either subvert them into satellites, as Soviet Russia did with Central and Eastern Europe; crush them in the course of their titanic struggle; or accept them as a bloc of equal force if they should succeed to unite themselves, as Western Europe did.

Around the middle of this century Europe was entering a new world. A world in which, within two generations, four billion people will be waging a losing battle against hunger and poverty, unless saved by a concerted effort of all. On the other hand, Europe was also entering an atomic world with its tremendous possibilities of industrial expansion, increased productivity and rising standards of living. A world of automation, of stepped up education and of the disappearance of still lingering class distinctions. Unless Europe rapidly adapted itself to the requirements of the technological age, it risked losing most of its political power, becoming within a generation a backward area and socially the remnant of an outlived feudal system.

The reforms which Europe needed had to be far reaching and had to encompass the sublimation of national frontiers consecrated by long and bloody wars, the assimilation of jealously guarded national customs and traditions of which the peoples were proud, the coordination of economies built by each nation individually, and the amalgamation of centuries old cultures.

The Miracle of Elasticity

The question was whether Europe could introduce these

reforms in time, whether its peoples had sufficient elasticity to readjust themselves psychologically and to cooperate in creating the necessary new conditions. Europe's problem was to find a response to the challenge posed by the fundamental changes in the world surrounding it. European nations were up against the combined forces of an outdated nationalism, deeply imbedded particularism and subversive Communism which could lead to its neutralization and from there to its gradual Communization. There was another danger, that of effacement. Britain, France, Germany, Italy and the smaller powers had to unite or they risked going the way of Spain and Portugal, who saw their empires crumble and had to continue to live in the shadow. But even these countries can rejuvenate themselves if they forget the past - Spain its authoritarianism of state and church, Portugal its dictatorial form of government and colonial possessions - and join the European integration.

Europe's remarkable recovery showed that it had the brains, the guts and the vision to rise to the occasion and reach the continental dimension, the power and industrial potential of the super-powers. Once on their way to recovery the nations of Western Europe were faced with a difficult choice. They had either to speed up their integration in view of the Communist danger, not only in Europe but also in Asia and Africa where it could threaten Europe from more than one side, or to slow down the process of unification over a longer period, from twelve to fifteen years, with the risk that growing prosperity and the absence of war would make it more difficult to overcome the formidable counterforces of inertia and nationalism. They chose the latter course and succeeded, greatly helped by the unrelenting pressure of the Kremlin, which time after time restored their unity.

Like every new concept, integration had its ups and downs. Dynamism in whatever form can never be a sustained forward effort. The greater the energy used, the sharper the ensuing reaction and temporary setbacks. Numerous were the times when a positive fulfilment seemed within grasp, only to be followed by a let-down, but in the end the efforts were justified. After Churchill's stirring appeal in The Hague in 1948 came the chilly reserve of the first meetings of the Council of Europe and Britain's negative attitude. After the swift ratification of the Schuman treaty and the high expectations resulting from it came the sudden backwash, the rejection of the European Defense Community and the interment of the European constitution and European Political Community. Then, after a two year lull in integration during 1954 and 1955 came the "relance européenne", the renewed drive towards unification culminating in the 1957 Treaty of Rome, establishing the two conerstones, the European Economic Community and Euratom. Ever since, economic integration has steadfastly increased until the Common Market changed Western Europe into a powerful trade bloc. From 1958-62 the internal trade of the Common Market doubled from 6.8 to 14 billion dollars and its external trade increased from 16 to 24 billion dollars. In the meantime the orientation towards a political union continues. To this end "Europe" already possesses a European Executive, the Council of Europe, a Legislative, the European Assembly and a Judiciary. Europe's integration which, fifteen years ago, seemed a chimera, has become a reality.

The opinion was rapidly gaining ground that once the Europe of the Six was firmly established, the Outer Seven would join it. President de Gaulle's veto of Britain was therefore a serious setback. This was partly due to his desire to make France the leading power of Europe - hence his pact of friendship with Germany—partly to break a presumed "Anglo-Saxon" hegemony over European affairs. Such obsession with France's grandeur is unlikely to survive de Gaulle, though it must be granted that Britain's exclusion from the Common Market was hailed by the extreme protagonists of European unification who long since had been concerned that Britain's traditional policy of compromise would endanger the "European spirit". This is the more so because Britain hesitated a long time between keeping up its association with the Commonwealth and its preferential tariffs or joining the Common Market. Britain's exclusion, which directly influences the attitude of the Outer Seven, may cause Europe's unification to lose its momentum. But provided that Britain still desires it, * its adherence can only be a question of time.

Until then European statesmen are unlikely to press for a

---

* The Labor Party expressed definite reservations as to Britain's entry into the Common Market.

too definite form of Europe's future political institutions in order to wait and see how the trend towards unification works out. At present there are two schools of thought. One envisages an as yet undefined union under a powerful European Parliament, no longer selected by national parliaments as the present European Assembly is, but by direct suffrage. The other leans towards de Gaulle's "Europe des Patries", which at best can become a kind of confederation, at worst an alliance with all the failings of the past. There is another reason why European statesmen refrain from finalizing their thinking about future political institutions. The ideas of Teilhard de Chardin, Julian Huxley and others made an impact, and many a statesman wishes to keep the political unification of Europe in step with what by now has come to be accepted as the inevitable unification of mankind as a whole.

The U.S. and Europe

Present American-European relations can best be understood by analyzing the ally whose attitude most deflects from the common course, namely that of France's President, Charles de Gaulle. A current criticism of his policy, which is often difficult to understand and aggravating to Americans, is to say that for lack of a more global motivation he justifies it as serving the greatness of France. That can hardly be doubted, but another way to look at de Gaulle is to see in him a compatriot of Teilhard de Chardin who bases his policy on a broad universal vision, but prefers to present it under the more easily acceptable guise of nationalism. In the U.S., de Gaulle's motivations are ascribed to pride, haughtiness and a certain single-mindedness as regards France's position in the world, though we ourselves do not always visualize the extent of the political transformations that are taking place around us. In trying to read de Gaulle's mind, one might come forward with the following hypotheses :

(1) Realizing the pressure to end the Cold War and the pull which the Common Market exercises on Eastern Europe, he concluded that the return of Russia to the European fold is only a matter of time. Moscow's split with China confirmed this view. Convinced that Russia will not take this step unless the American presence disappears from Europe, he

seeks to disassociate Europe from the United States.

(2) In order to achieve this he wants to build the Common Market around a French-German nucleus and to keep Britain out of continental Europe's inner councils.

(3) Developing this vision, he realises that a rapprochement between Russia and this kind of Europe inevitably must lead to Russian supremacy over the continent unless France - and eventually Germany? - has a nuclear force of its own. Hence his insistence on his "force de frappe" which he, moreover, claims because no self-respecting power can leave the vital decision of its nuclear defense to another nation.

(4) That is why he insists on freeing France from its dependence on American nuclear power. He is not absolutely convinced that if Europe is attacked, Washington will push the nuclear button and risk the annihilation of its cities. The need for his own nuclear force increases, since Britain, relying on the American retaliatory force, gave up its Skybolts in exchange for Polaris submarines. This, by the way, irked De Gaulle and may have been one of his reasons for barring England's entry into the Common Market.

(5) De Gaulle wants European unity but in his own way, namely not under American auspices. But in European eyes his idea of a "Europe des Patries" is too nationalistic, too obviously aimed at giving France a position of hegemony, and too much conceived in terms of the past to be in keeping with modern developments.

(6) De Gaulle's excursions in the Far-East, Latin America and sooner or later Soviet Russia represent an effort to restore French prestige in these parts of the world and counterbalance the political influence of the U.S. His reason for recognizing Red China may have been that the U.S. may sooner or later have to do the same, and that he prefers to precede Washington than to follow in its wake.

In all these matters de Gaulle's attitude may be traced back to the United States' refusal to heed his request for an allied directorate of the United States, Britain and France. He looked upon this as a personal slight and as disparaging to the prestige of France. This, on top of some unfortunate incidents during the war, are the real reasons underlying the present strain in our relations with France. The adverse reaction this creates in other European countries merely increases his obstinacy. He saw in the U.S. replacement of its bases in Turkey and Italy by Polaris submarines an indication of Washington's decision to one-sidedly define its policy towards the Soviet Union. During the Cuba crisis, and notwithstanding the fact that he whole-heartedly supported the United States' stand, he pointedly remarked that Washington had informed but not consulted its European allies.

De Gaulle shares the concern of other Western European nations about an eventual understanding between the United States and the Soviet Union. Should this ultimately be reached, the super-powers might be tempted to use their combined military and industrial predominance to subject the remainder of the world to their will. These fears are, for this reason alone, unfounded: that should the super-powers thus "find" each other in infamy, the inexorable result of such crude power politics could but be that one would ultimately attempt to destroy the other. A lasting rapprochement can only be reached by common adherence to a concept that transcends both ideologies, on a level that would preclude the use of power and instead require a global cooperation between the U.S. and U.S.S.R. in all human fields and one in which the allies must necessarily become involved. Once the worst suspicion has been allayed between the United States and the Soviet Union, there is hope that international relations will be envisaged from the point of view of the whole of mankind and no longer from that of the two superpowers.

The President of France did not draw, or did not wish to draw these logical conclusions, but continues to follow a deliberate policy of disengagement with the U.S. In many ways this clashes with the foreseeable course of events. He may interrupt Europe's integration; he cannot stop it because the movement towards continental entities is irresistible. He may hope to bring along a French inspired mediation between the United States and Russia; he forgets that if the chips are down the Soviet Union will deal directly with the United States. The future lies in an ultimate convergence and cooperation of the free and Communist worlds. This can only be reached through a number of intermediary stages but not by a return to past concepts as de Gaulle suggests.

As to his inroads in the Far-East, his proposal of neutralizing South Vietnam in order to restore peace to that region before possible North-South tensions reach a climax, is farsighted, even if he lacks the means and power to see it through. What is to be retained from De Gaulle's views is the desirability of putting the N.A.T.O. alliance on a broader basis. What must be rejected is his contention that an independent Europe is more in line with future developments than an interdependent Atlantic Community. However, to achieve the latter all creative forces of the Western alliance have to be mobilized in an effort at total cooperation. This does not mean that the U.S. has to accede to De Gaulle's demand for a directorate. At least, not in this peremptory form, but close cooperation between the United States, Britain, France and Germany is likely to exercise a considerable influence in the world, especially if based on a philosophy that involves the totality of mankind and which stems from the old continent itself.

N.A.T.O.

In a fast changing world in which the raging ideological struggle may ere long dissipate, a military alliance solely based on containing an opponent who no longer is an enemy must lose its momentum. Such an alliance, unless thoroughly revised and basically remolded, becomes a source of friction and clashes.

If the signs point towards a growing cooperation between the opponents in the Cold War, how much more necessary is it to achieve between allied nations a close cooperation which transcends the military sphere and comes to grips with civilian problems of world importance. This requires collaboration of the best brains in the Western world. What is most needed today are political leaders of stature and with vision. Had De Gaulle been encouraged by the alliance to bring into play his historical sense and political foresight, this would have benefitted the common good. A more flexible cooperation with him might have prevented his demand for participating in such an unwieldy body as a formal directorate, and saved the U.S. the embarrassment of a refusal. What we did was to deflect his thinking from the Western world to concentrate on the interests of France alone. An example of how a potentially valuable contribution is sacrificed to a too rigid conception of our N.A.T.O. alliance.

Had it been widened from a purely military to a political,

economic and social organization, as Paul Henri Spaak and other European statesmen hoped it would, N.A.T.O. would at present be a powerful instrument for dealing with a number of world-wide problems. It could have evolved a common philosophy in the fight against Communism instead of following divergent and sometimes contradictory approaches in, for example, matters of trade. Or it could have reached a unified attitude in matters of foreign help to the new countries * or a common approach to such problems as poverty and the disparity between haves and have-nots all over the world. An extended N.A.T.O. could play an important role in overcoming the Cold War and continuing the détente between the free and Communist worlds by bringing home to the Communists the functional need of individual freedom in the scheme of evolution, and to the free world the moral value of collective service as an attribute of that living organism, mankind. In such a N.A.T.O. the U.S. and Europe could complement each other in a remarkable way. For the U.S. renews itself in action and advances pragmatically from case to case, while Europe represents a state of mind which incessantly questions its every achievement, whether scientific or social, and thus renews itself in the spirit.

By combining these two approaches the alliance could deal with all problems in a decisive and yet detached way. Misunderstandings as between the United States and France arose because we reversed the order of priority in our relationship. Instead of following the lead given by the Marshall Plan and continuing to give top priority to political and economic matters as the means of building a viable world, we made military containment practically the sole objective of the alliance, thus reverting to a recipe of the past. By persisting in military containment as our chief means of counterbalancing Communism, we oversimplified

---

* Europe revealed two interesting facts to the U.S. It proved that the right kind of economic help at the right time can work miracles, and that such help cannot only restore a people's vital energies as in Britain, France and the Lowlands, but also its commonsense, even after the most intense indoctrination, as in Germany. If ever the concept of foreign aid was vindicated as an instrument of foreign policy, it was in Europe after the war.

an extremely complex situation. Just as the role of the
United States' deterrent is to prevent nuclear war, the
military role of N.A.T.O. should have been restricted to
establishing an equilibrium of conventional forces in Europe.
Since the Cold War is more and more shifting from the
military to the political field, the Western alliance's main
attention should have been focused on the latter. Had N.A.T.O.
done this, it might already have been able to overcome the
Cold War and lay a solid foundation for a viable Atlantic
Community.

S.E.A.T.O. and C.E.N.T.O. are at present purely military
alliances. As we and our partners in them belong to different
forms of civilization, they can less easily be extended to
political, economic and social fields. Nevertheless their
transformation, though necessarily slower than that of
N.A.T.O. should equally be pursued. Within a growing world
solidarity and world economy, civilizations are automatically
converging as all of us can observe, * and gradually cooperation with our allies in the Far and Middle East in non-
military matters will become as necessary as that with our
Western allies.

The Atlantic Community

We mentioned that close collaboration with our Western
allies would facilitate the advent of an Atlantic Community.
President Kennedy hailed it as one of the future goals of
American diplomacy, and many European statesmen are
looking towards such a development. Its advantages would be
manifold. It could serve as a bastion of freedom, liberalize
trade over large areas and usher in a new era of world
cooperation. It could, moreover, be helpful in reaching out
beyond the present stage of continental blocs by creating
an intercontinental area and bringing the world a step
nearer to the general convergence of mankind.

In January, 1962, a N.A.T.O.'s citizen convention came
forward with some concrete proposals. They recommended
the establishment of a High Council as Executive of the

* Manufacturing processes fuse, large cities such as Tokyo
and New York begin to look alike, and conformity in clothing
and other ways of living increase everywhere.

Atlantic Community to deal with common political problems, a Consultative Assembly and an Atlantic Court of Justice. These proposals followed the pattern used for Europe's integration. The most delicate problem facing both organizations is the part of national sovereignty to be transferred to them. It is too early to take into consideration what at a later stage will become self-evident, namely that in large communities sovereignty belongs to all the people irrespective of their nationality, and must be exercised by their directly chosen executive, legislative and judiciary organs.

For the time being, and though Anglo-Saxons prefer to define political rights and obligations in precise terms, the overall organization of the Atlantic Community cannot be firmly outlined and must be left to find its own practical level. What matters is that efforts at further unification remain in line with the direction of man's evolution. If the peoples of the Atlantic Community adopt the modern concepts of evolution, they will be able to generate a spiritual force sufficiently strong to create a world-wide following and a vision appealing enough to even convince the Communists.

Chapter XVII

THE U.S. AND COMMUNIST COUNTRIES

The U.S. and East Asia

Red China

If the U.S. uses persuasion to end the Cold War with Soviet Russia, the question arises what attitude it must assume towards Red China. There are no indications that Peking is in any way open to discussions with Washington, as was suggested for Soviet Russia. There remains the decision whether or not to recognize the Mao Government. Long after the U.S. and its allies have understood that the Cold War cannot be won by military means, it stubbornly continues to follow a policy of armed containment against Red China. Apart from this, there is the United States' loyalty to the National Government in Taipeh, our war-time ally. At the time of writing both the recognition of Red China with its admission to the United Nations, and the war in South Vietnam are problems of current interest. Their solutions cannot be long postponed. If approached in the new spirit which is slowly breaking through in the U.S., as voiced by Senator Fulbright, the Chairman of the Foreign Relations Commission, Washington will soon have to base its policy on facts and not on sentiments. The facts are (1) that Chiang Kai Shek lacks the power and probably the response on the mainland needed to liberate it, (2) that Red China's admission to the U.N. will exacerbate the rift with Russia if the two are confronted on the same forum instead of exchanging abuses from a distance, and (3) that isolation breeds fanaticism and that the sooner a people like the Chinese come into contact with others, the sooner they may recognize that their prejudices towards the West are unfounded, especially as regards the U.S., which in the past always supported the cause of China. If we can convince the people of China that we are not hostile to them and if we treat them with due consideration, a great deal of their hatred and desire to overcompensate for a century of inferiority is likely to disappear. The most practical way to end Red China's isolation is to restore normal political and commercial ties with it, as most of our allies did. Unless one deals with a nation one cannot hope to sway it. Once again we have to remind ourselves that ideas cannot be combatted with guns in a nuclear age.

South-Vietnam

This equally applies to the war in Vietnam. This war seems to have become a matter of prestige rather than of reason. The question is whether the U.S. is not hesitating between two opinions. Asked for military hardware and advisers by the South-Vietnam government, it ended by getting mixed up in the actual fighting in line with the concept of containment. In view of the Viet Cong's armed attacks on South-Vietnam, the U.S. feels justified in repulsing force by force. We consider it our duty to help the countries of South-East Asia in maintaining their freedom against Communism. In doing this we assume that North-Vietnam is a satellite of Red China bent on spreading Communism and opposed to being neutral. We further assume that unless the U.S. pours more money and men into South-Vietnam, it is likely to turn neutral, which will unavoidably lead to its being overrun by the Viet Cong and incorporated behind the Bamboo Curtain.

But many of these "a priori" assumptions are doubtful. Are the peoples of South-East Asia prepared to rally to the cause either of freedom or of Communism? It is more likely that the ideological problem is of little interest to them and that they prefer to be left to themselves in order to solve their problems in their own way. It is still an open question as to whether the South-Vietnamese people are willing to take up arms at the instance of the U.S. Up to the moment of writing only South-Vietnamese governments have expressed their willingness to fight. A succession of military coups does not necessarily denote a popular will to fight, but rather a desire of the leaders to bolster their power with the help of American aid and support. If North-Vietnam is the same kind of Red Chinese satellite as Albania, it is more a matter of financial support than of political conviction. It is equally uncertain that South-Vietnam's neutrality would push it into the Communist camp. Laos and Cambodia became neutral, and though at times they have showed Communist leanings, they still are neutral.

Should the U.S. insist on first beating down the Viet Cong, it will have to resort to retaliatory raids in order to give Ho Chi Minh a taste of his own medecine. But if the U.S. succeeds in beating off the Viet Cong, will it be possible to inculcate in the South-Vietnamese the toughness to further hold out against subversion after our departure? Far Easterners excel in the art of negotiation and see in compromise the beginning and end of all wisdom. Every statesman in the Far East likes to try his hand at the game, not unrewarding, of playing upon the East-West struggle. It even seems uncertain that the U.S. can convince the Vietnamese people to wage an all-out Communist war, as they may rather prefer to come to terms with North-Vietnam. In any case the fact of our forcing an anti-Communist war on people who prefer to compromise would make it difficult for the men in the Kremlin to hold on to a policy of rationalism. American diplomacy sees in any change of our policy a danger of weakening South-Vietnamese morale, but with Far-Eastern people it is necessary to deal in the Oriental and not in the Western way.

President Johnson once said that he would have no objection to the neutralization of South-Vietnam provided that North-Vietnam would equally be neutralized. But Washington never seriously tried to obtain North-Vietnam's neutrality. If both South and North-Vietnam could come to terms they would stop fighting, though they might still go through the motions in order to collect from their respective protectors. It is doubtful whether North-Vietnam would go out of its way to have South-Vietnam become Communist. A Red-Chinese take-over of the whole of Indo-China would be as distasteful to Ho Chi Minh as to the Soviet rulers. Incidentally, the U.S. would not lose face in Far Eastern eyes if it agreed of its own accord to some kind of understanding between the two Vietnams; it would only lose face if forced to end its intervention.

Looking ahead, it seems to be in the United States' and in the world's interest to put an end to the fighting in Indo-China instead of trying to obtain a solution by force. We already remarked * that a change from East-West to North-South tensions is in the making. In an effort to gain the support of as many unaligned nations as possible, Chou En Lai worked towards this end on his travels through Asia and Africa. Should the ideological fight resolve itself into a struggle for the equalization of living standards all over the world, this would help China to gain the lead in the Communist movement by replacing the present ideological squabble between Peking and Moscow with a new departure in the world-wide struggle to help the underdog. One of the first objectives of the have-nots would be to undo any solution imposed by force in that region by the United States.

President De Gaulle's advice to neutralize South-Vietnam and his offer of assistance to that country together with his renewal of trade relations with Hanoi, appears in a new light. Besides being prompted by the desire for re-establishing France's influence in that part of the world, it may also have been offered as a means to pacify the Indo-Chinese region before the North-South tensions reach a climax. If the U.S. could replace its one-sided preoccupation with South-Vietnam with an effort to establish an economically viable, even if politically disinterested, region, this might prove the best way to restrict China's influence, besides being more in line with the general political trend of the future. An American initiative in convening a conference of all interested countries would be hailed as an act of leadership. A recognition of Red China would further clarify and strengthen the U.S. position, for it is not by clinging to a policy out of the past but by coming forward with a new plan that the future can be safeguarded.

Should the Viet Cong continue to attack after neutralization of the whole region, the U.S. would be fully justified in using military means in order to prevent an upset in the existing power balance. An "a priori" assumption that neutralization will automatically lead to Communization is what weakens our present moral position.

The U.S. and the Satellites

The U.S. has a special interest in the satellites. These

---

* Cf. Chapter XIII, page 161.

countries knew freedom before they were forced under the Communist yoke. For many years they looked to the U.S. as the only country able to save them from their plight. They have in this country National Councils, a kind of unofficial governments-in-exile, and strong lobbies composed of former compatriots who in the past emigrated to the U.S. For a time the administration in Washington was under the illusion that it might be instrumental in their liberation. Then it became clear that this was impossible in a nuclear age. East Berlin and Hungary were tragedies for the satellite nations and shocking disappointments to the Americans. Political firebrands may still ask what hope of freedom there remains for the satellites; both they and the U.S. realise that freedom cannot be restored by revolution or war but only by such a process of gradual transformation as is taking place in these countries today.

The role they are beginning to play is that of a laboratory-like experiment in which, through force of circumstances, two hostile ideologies slowly but inevitably converge. On the one hand they use Communism to overcome the inequalities of their not so distant feudal era. On the other hand they turn to Western Europe partly through natural inclination, partly to gain more independence from a Comecon (Communist Council for Mutual Economic Assistance) which stifles their national aspirations. They have the tendency to ascribe every deviation from Communism to feelings of nationalism, but in many instances their policy is dictated by a collective attraction to the Common Market and an urge, perhaps not fully realized, to build a bridge between the Soviet Union and Western Europe. The time may come when Soviet Russia itself seeks some tie-up with the Common Market. Within the Comecon bloc Russia can maintain a reasonable economic growth, but when it comes to catching up with the U.S. economy, it must export. It cannot afford to lose the Western European market and must come to terms with the Common Market. In the meantime the satellites are the ones which urge the Kremlin to break with Red China and seek a rapprochement with the West.

Much of what happens in the satellites goes against the grain of American thinking. They no longer clamor for freedom or condemn Communism, but rather keep aloof from ideological problems. They direct their economic activities

towards the West without shouting it over the rooftops. They
are evolving something new, while observing a strict Communist discipline, without, however, adopting the faceless
Communist conformity and while still maintaining some
characteristic traits of their own.

Poland is the most defiant. Strongly nationalistic, it openly
sticks to its Catholic faith and has steadfastly refused
collectivization of its agriculture.* It maintains a considerable degree of freedom in art and literature as well as
in social experiments. The Polish leaders rationalized the
situation, and though at times they stand up to the Kremlin,
they have achieved a close association with the Soviet Union.
The same applies in a greater or lesser degree to all the
satellites.

Czechoslovakia, fully industrialized before the Communist
take-over, at the same time both enforced a model Communist
work code and sabotaged Comecon planning based on cheap
buying of Czech industrial products in exchange for highly
priced Russian raw materials and shoddy goods. Prague
opened its doors wide to Western tourists and, following the
Kafka tradition, to Western modernism.

Hungary has regained some of the elegance and gaiety of
pre-war days. Notwithstanding its basic poverty, it imports
Western luxury goods with the same unconcern its pleasure-
loving aristocracy displayed in feudal days. Hungarians have
achieved a remarkable degree of non conformism and avant-
gardism. The regime liberally accords permits for foreign
travel, even to the West. All this strengthens the people's
self-assurance.

Rumania is the most "dégagé" of the satellites. With their
quick intelligence the Rumanians gave a Latin twist to the
ponderous Communist planning. Their keen managers and
technicians, out for results, cut through the mass of bureaucratic obstructions. Relying on the relative freedom of
movement which its self-sufficiency accords to their large
petroleum industry, they turn to the West for equipment for
new industrial ventures in the chemical and other fields.
Rumania does not hesitate to come forward with social
innovations such as the workers' councils which Khrushchev
declared were worth studying.

* Only fifteen per cent of the land is collectivized.

East Germany is practically still occupied territory. Post-war reparations levied by the Soviet Government and the six million East Germans who fled to the West greatly weakened its economy. However, the people remain thoroughly German and if, in the course of time, East and West Germany converge, as they are likely to, the progress of integration will be smoother and more soundless than is at present expected.

All this could not have happened if Khrushchev, aware of the explosive danger which the satellites present, had not decided to give them more leeway. He apparently considered the buffer they form, the evidence they furnish that other Western nations can adopt Communism, their support against China, and the bridge they can build to Western Europe as more important than their toeing the party line.

The U.S. can help this "opening towards freedom" by increasing American trade and aid to the satellites. The once prevalent idea that refusal of aid and trade are the better tools to combat Communism is on the way to being abandoned as over-simplified and as belonging to an age that is no longer in tune with present developments. The economy of the satellites is likely to get increasingly integrated with that of Western Europe, and thereby to facilitate the transformation of Communism. Inexorable changes are taking place, perhaps too slowly to be detected by the untrained eye, but with a pace considerably faster than a decade ago.

The U.S. and Cuba

Castro's Cuba has been referred to in previous chapters. This bridgehead of Communism in the Western hemisphere is a thorn in the United States' side, and it costs Washington more self-control to be rational about the situation over there than in all other Communist countries. The popular slogan of "send the Marines in" strongly savors of the past and the Cuban problem sharply divides those who have learned to think ahead and those who, oblivious of changes, blissfully float in days gone by. Though, generally speaking, trade can play an important role in overcoming Communism, it was right for the U.S. to break off all trade relations with Cuba after its confiscation of American property without compensation. To ask others to break off trade relations is another matter and one which can too easily be viewed as interference. Unless situations such as the Cuban one can be ruled by internationally accepted laws, they raise a delicate issue.

In the absence of a regular international police force, it is sometimes necessary for a great power to assume police functions. History abounds of examples of the benefit the world has reaped from such policing under the Pax Romana, Britannica, Franca, etc., when the armies and navies of great powers maintained law and order in various parts of the world. Had the U.S. been able to openly act in Cuba on behalf of itself and others, its intervention would have been justified. As it happened, the countries of Latin America would have been more uneasy about an American intervention than relieved by the removal of the Communist threat from the Western hemisphere. The compromise decision to act under the screen of "volunteers", and then half-heartedly, could only end in failure. The Bay of Pigs miscalculation was furthermore due to excessive optimism of Cuban refugees who mistook their dreams for reality. A victorious invading army may cause local populations to rise, as happened when the Ukrainians revolted after the German invasion,* but to count on an uprising in the wake of the landing of an insignificant force was unrealistic. Castro will go the way of all Latin American dictators who bring their countries to the verge of economic disaster, and such an end will be more effective than one forced by U.S. intervention.

---

* When Hitler committed another of his monumental blunders by acting as the conqueror instead of the liberator.

Chapter XVIII

THE U.S. AND THE U.S.S.R.

Relationship with the Soviet Union

The nearly fifty years of relationship between the United States and the Soviet Union went through a number of extreme phases. Both countries have in common that they started, so to say, from scratch after their respective revolutions. When they wrote their Constitution Americans were in the fortunate position of not being burdened by a political heritage, while the Russians made up their mind to bury the past and begin with a clean slate. But while the U.S. periodically adapted itself to the changing times, amending its Constitution and readjusting society when the need arose, the Bolshevik revolution was hampered after the initial overthrow by the limitations of its Marxist-Leninist dogma to which it clung with a fervor worthy of the most reactionary cause. It follows that we, and not the Russians, should be regarded as the revolutionaries of our time. However, a change appeared in the offing when Khrushchev, gripped by something like Kennedy's urge to reach out for new frontiers, moved in the direction of greater understanding for the needs of his people and the problems of mankind as a whole.

The U.S. did not recognize the Soviet Union during the first sixteen years of its existence, which did not prevent it from giving large-scale aid to Russia under the Hoover Plan. When the totalitarian nature of the Soviet Government became increasingly apparent, relations dropped to freezing point. Recognition in 1933 did not greatly improve matters. For some time an effort was made to get Russia on the side of the allies when the Nazi threat of war drew nearer. The Stalin-Ribbentrop pact incensed American public opinion, and a hostile feeling persisted until the day that Hitler's folly brought the United States and Soviet Union into the same camp. We became allies and under the mellowing influence of a common cause, and against our better judgment, we

abandoned ourselves to the illusion that Communism was
slowly veering towards democracy. The cold-blooded annexation of Eastern Europe and Stalin's breach of faith when
he went back on his promise to hold free elections in the
satellite countries, brought a revulsion of Western feeling.
From an ally the Soviet Government turned into America's
number one enemy, and for a decade all the fear and loathing
of the American people was concentrated on Soviet Communism. Hatred threatened to turn into hysteria when McCarthy
and other demagogues of the extreme right, frustrated by
the impossibility of getting at the enemy, substituted a wild-
goose chase against Communists and presumed Communists
within the U.S. for an attack on Communism across the ocean.

As if all these ups and downs were not enough, the last
decade introduced a number of imponderables into American-
Russian relations which worked at cross purposes. Russian
efforts to have their European annexations accepted by the
free world were countered by American rearmament and
Point IV and Marshall Plans. American hope of being able to
exercise sufficient pressure by means of its atomic monopoly
ended when Russian scientists caught up with us. The Kremlin's efforts to overwhelm the free world by a display of
power and by nuclear blackmail failed, but so did our plans
to roll back Communism and liberate the satellites. The
Russians tried to bleed the U.S. white by forcing it into
enormous defense and space expenditures which did produce
a drain on our gold reserves. But hardly had this happened
when their design boomeranged, and it was the Soviet Union
which had to drop out of the moon race, curtail its military
expenses and dip into its gold reserves for the purchase of
wheat in Western markets. All this was accompanied by an
endless series of larger or smaller crises followed by
temporary relaxations welcomed by the free world but also
by the Russian people who responded with recurrent bursts
of sympathy for the U.S.

Fundamentally there is nothing strange in all these imponderables in Russo-American relations. When Europeans
began their migration to the new world, they were fleeing
from unbearable authoritative pressures at home and in
search of freedom and the reassertion of their personality.
This longing for individual liberty was to put its stamp on the
next two centuries of American life. In Russia it was the

opposite. There the movement was not to reassert individualism but to eliminate it as the symbol of a hated past. Collectivity became the all-encompassing objective. In this manner environmental influences were able for a long period to upset the equilibrium between the two opposing principles of individual freedom and collectivity and the nations which embodied them, and the appearance of so many imponderables was nature's effort to restore the balance. The result seems to be that both sides are finally driven to a policy of accommodation which may eventually lead to cooperation. *

United States' Policy towards the Soviet Union

The seesawing events of the past suggest the lack of a clearcut and consistent United States' policy towards the Communist countries. Looking back to the post-war period it is indeed difficult to detect a logical line in it. Washington never defined any precise objectives with the exception of John Foster Dulles' fixed idea about the unrighteousness of Communism and his self-appointed role of protector of freedom and avenger of Communist outrages. Dulles may have hoped to restore free governments in the European satellites and Chiang Kai Shek's power over the mainland of China, but beyond the use of slogans such as "massive retaliation", "liberation" and "brinkmanship" he never indicated by what means this policy could be enacted. President Eisenhower held sounder views but found it equally difficult to formulate his somewhat vague notions of statecraft into a precise foreign program. **

Meanwhile the administration encouraged an ambitious program of privately organized counter-propaganda directed at the European nations behind the Iron Curtain. The aim of the Free Europe Committee and its subsidiary Radio Free Europe was to keep alive a spirit of freedom in the satellite

---

* Dr. David Pimentel, biologist of Cornell University, explains that "evolution favors species that get along with each other". He reached this conclusion — with its interesting implication for mankind — after experiments proved that house flies and blow flies, after cycles of alternate dominance, learn to coexist in peace and harmony.

** Cf. "The Ordeal of Power" by Emmet John Hughes.

countries, but Washington never prepared any plans for what action to take if a revolution broke out in these countries. When in 1953 there were rebellions in Czechoslovakia and East Berlin, and in 1956 a full-fledged revolution broke out in Hungary, the U.S. did nothing. True, the Hungarians revolted at a moment when the attention of the U.S. was riveted on the final stage of Eisenhower's second election campaign, and when a combined Israeli-British-French attack on Suez took place with its dangerous possibility of breaking up the alliance. Russia's savage repression represented no attack on the Europe of our allies, and thus massive retaliation was not set in motion. Apart from this consideration, the U.S. had insufficient conventional forces for an intervention, and even had these been available, they could not have reached Hungary except by violating Austria's neutrality. So the U.S. kept aloof and had to look away while the very freedom it advocated was crucified.

This observation is no plea for American armed intervention, it only serves to draw attention to the United States' wavering policy towards the Soviet Union. How wavering it is, is more clearly shown when compared to its attitude "vis-à-vis" our British and French allies in their attack against Nasser. While leaving it to the United Nations to deal with the Hungarian tragedy, Washington exerted direct pressure on Britain and France to stop their invasion of Egypt. In itself, this attitude may have been correct, but it gave the impression that the United States was applying different yardsticks in similar eventualities.

Another vagueness in American foreign policy faced it with a different danger. Though Republicans had criticized Dean Acheson for not clearly defining a line of demarcation beyond which the U.S. would not permit any Communist inroad into the existing balance of power, and rightly related this to the Korean war, the Eisenhower administration equally neglected to indicate where Communist penetration would lead to American armed intervention. Generally speaking, Washington had never conceived, since the outbreak of the Cold War, of an overall plan for setting into motion all levers of pressure against the Soviet Union and simultaneously mobilizing world public opinion for a concerted effort at presenting an alternative to the senseless ideological struggle.

This changed under the Kennedy administration. Perception

deepened, and a line of action was gradually mapped out. At the onset, things were still vague. The only fixed point was that as long as the power situation remained in equilibrium, neither of the two opponents could impose its will on the other, with the likelihood that international tensions could be kept under control. As this did not tie in with the Kremlin's policy which, by a combination of bluff and manipulation tried to create the impression of superior power, the U.S. had constantly to remain on the defensive in the Berlin and similar crises. American public opinion, too long alerted about the Soviet "danger", failed to fully rationalize the situation. It was insufficiently aware of the Kremlin's intent to avoid nuclear war and saw in the United States' defensive posture an indication of Soviet superiority. It insisted through Congress on higher defense expenditures than the government deemed necessary and clamored for greater militancy. It was up to President Kennedy to convince the country of the sober fact that the United States' deterrent, provided it is kept up-to-date, serves to prevent and not to wage nuclear war, and that to think otherwise would be to play in the hands of Soviet bluff and blackmail.

The crucial test was soon to come which would prove whether the Kremlin had definitely abandoned the idea of nuclear war in the face of American determination to defend its vital interests, one of which is to oppose a one-sided disruption of the balance of power. In Cuba a situation arose in which the United States, though having itself surrounded the Soviet Union with military bases, had to demand the dismantling of the Cuban base on account of the one, inadmissible fact that it upset an already precarious balance of power. At the time of this first direct confrontation between the U.S. and the U.S.S.R. the impression prevailed that Washington might have been confident that the Kremlin would not risk nuclear war but that it was not sure whether considerations of prestige or pressure by the Red Army might not force Khrushchev into a desperate bluff with incalculable consequences.

As the administration had not beforehand defined American positions upon which no Soviet encroachment would be tolerated, it can be assumed that it had made no preparations to counter such an eventuality. Consequently the success of Kennedy's riposte was not so much due to an anticipatory plan as to a brilliant improvisation at a moment of extreme tension.

It was Kennedy's further merit that after this initial period of probing, the United States' policy towards Russia adopted a more consistent line. He saw that only a breakthrough in political thinking can lead to a lasting détente and apparently found in Khrushchev a certain understanding of this point of view. The kind of understanding that can only arise in a peasant so deeply confident in his instinct and at the same time so outstandingly intelligent as to be able to weave an aggressive psychological foreign policy, an understanding for values that transcend this very policy, together with a controversial policy of concessions to the Russian people, into a single pattern. The result of Kennedy's new departure was an effort to open up channels whereby conflicts can be solved by rationalization instead of force.

The first concrete steps were the test ban and the establishment of a "hot line" between Washington and Moscow. This is logically to lead to further understandings about how to prevent surprise attacks and what initial steps to undertake in the matter of disarmament, for no lasting relaxation can be obtained unless both parties embody their endeavors into common accords. To achieve this it is necessary, as we have already remarked, to initiate a cooperation with the Russians in as many fields as possible, in science, space, technology, trade, agriculture and especially in problems that concern the whole world. This will produce an atmosphere in which the Cold War automatically recedes into the background. What matters is to get cooperation going, even if it is done haltingly, hesitantly, imperfectly, as long as there is a beginning. It is only after a period of cooperation that one can hope to reach a worthwhile stage of disarmament.

Disarmament

At first disarmament is likely to be a will-o'-the-wisp as difficult to seize as a ray of light and as elusive as a dream. At best it can only be achieved in painfully slow stages.

Technically speaking, a spiralling armaments race carries in itself the danger of war. The fact that millions of people are concentrated on warfare cannot but promote an aggressive mentality. Enormous amounts of capital are invested in military hardware which becomes continually outdated, calling for new capital outlays, and such waste without any results to show, produces feelings of frustration.

The Communists manufactured nuclear and conventional arms at first to gain world domination and now partly out of fear of growing American superiority, partly for purposes of negotiating from strength and creating an image of invincibility, while the free world manufactures them as a deterrent against war. A most costly method for creating and opposing an illusion.

Lately the Soviet Government has had to invest more capital in agriculture in order to prevent internal unrest and discontent. This necessitates in the long run a drastic cutback in military expenses. The Kremlin is therefore inclined to a measure of disarmament. This may at first seem illogical because in a disarmed world the Kremlin would be deprived of its most important instrument of pressure. On second thought and given the Communist leaders' exuberant faith in their system, the men of the Kremlin may well believe that a disarmed free world may more easily be bullied and manipulated and, moreover, that deprived of the stimulus of huge armament orders, the West is likely to founder in a series of depressions and economic crises. Besides that, general disarmament would make it difficult for Red China to become a nuclear power and would thus diminish the threat on China's Eastern border and the Soviet obsession with encirclement. It would likewise eliminate the spread of nuclear armament to other powers.

As to the free world, disarmament would mean the end of Communist nuclear blackmail. It would gain the U.S. the sympathy of the world at large and of the new nations which, unaware of the Communist double talk when they propose total disarmament under unacceptable conditions, do not understand our insistence to remain fully armed. Disarmament would enable the free world to spur its scientific and industrial endeavors to undreamt heights, to raise the levels of education at home and all over the world, to grant large-scale assistance to all needy countries, to combat poverty and disease and to stimulate world trade. And with all these tasks in the offing, the free world no longer needs armament as an economic regulator.

In Communist eyes, disarmament could divert large funds into research and space exploration and thus raise Communist prestige. Part of the money could be used to improve living conditions and to encourage the labor force of the Soviet Union to increase its efforts to overtake the American economy. Disarmament would be impossible without an adequate international police force and consequently without strengthening the United Nations. Both the issues of disarmament and United Nations run parallel and are closely connected. Whether disarmament can be obtained under the rule of law depends on the authority which the Communist world is prepared to grant to the United Nations.

In the past all efforts at disarmament failed on account of the Kremlin's stubborn resistance to control. There may have been a genuine desire on both sides of the Iron Curtain to end the arms' race, but in a closed society suspicion assumes such paranoic proportions, especially in a Russia with its centuries old tradition of secrecy, that there is little hope of overcoming it. In view of the Soviet Union's past treaty violations, it is understandable that the free world is unwilling to conclude disarmament agreements without adequate controls. The question is whether the free world can find means other than local control which are sufficiently adequate, and even more important is the alternative of either disarming without fully adequate control or not disarming at all. In the nuclear test ban the United States for the first time took a chance, and it still remains a question whether it may be able to drop some of its original absolutecontrol demands. For it is not unlikely that a change in the psychological climate resulting from disarmament in stages offers a greater safeguard than the most precise control. When this book appears, a cooling off period may have either given Russia the time for a change of mind or the United States the conviction that adequate control can be exercised without sending inspectors into the Soviet Union. It can, in any case, be assumed that negotiations and conversations held in the meantime have contributed in dispelling at least some of the mutual suspicion between the two countries.

The energy, brains and money that can be switched from armaments to more constructive endeavours are likely to stir up mankind to new exploits compared with which the ideological strife sinks into insignificance.

Soviet Foreign Policy

Since the end of World War II Soviet foreign policy has been conducted, if not with more foresight, in any case with more vigor and premeditation than American foreign policy. We described Russian psychological warfare, its efforts at eroding anti-Soviet alliances and at demoralizing the free world and luring nations into neutralism. This policy seemed to pay off until a few years ago. The change came on account of Soviet internal difficulties but also as a result of the United States' realization of its missile superiority coupled to a growing insight into the facts that the Soviet bark was worse than its bite, that the dire threats of nuclear annihilation were a means of intimidation and that the Kremlin was as eager as the United States to avoid nuclear war. The change also coincided with the Kremlin's awareness of the Russian people's peace-loving nature, which is not conducive to warlike adventures. This is due to their subconscious desire for better understanding with the rest of the world, and strengthened by Russia's own peace propaganda, the Kremlin being unable to exorcise the spirit it has evoked.

Some Americans see in the present relaxation no more than a phase in the Kremlin's psychological warfare preceding a new period of aggression. And they would be right if, as a result of a temporary détente, we were to weaken our defense, thus inviting the Soviet Union to new acts of aggression. The problem confronting the United States at present is to devise a policy under the assumption that the West is not going to let down its guard but will maintain its full defensive power and nevertheless continue to press for relaxation. The problem is thus narrowed down to what tactics and what attitude to assume for engaging the Soviet Union in non-militant and non-dogmatic conversations in which both sides avoid fanaticism and follow the road of reason from which there is no easy return.

An American-Russian Dialogue

In a dialogue with the Russians our goal must be to divert their thinking from the Cold War and guide it towards the basic problems that face mankind and that are caused by the present crisis in its evolution. There already were indications that Khrushchev's thinking did transcend the narrow confines of the Cold War, and that all that was needed was to give it a scientific foundation compatible with Marxist theory.

Why Talk to Communists?

After nearly two decades of Cold War many people doubt the use of any conversation with the Russians. Some, unable to understand why the world, after having destroyed Nazi tyranny, cannot end the intolerable red totalitarianism in the same way, overlooks two irrefutable considerations. The first is that to destroy Communism requires a nuclear war which could simultaneously destroy the free world. The second is that National Socialism was based on a myth of Wagnerian vagueness, on the return of the medieaval imperial tradition of the Hohenstauffen* and on an idolization of German racism, aggravated by the inferiority complex of a people always ordered around and never educated to think independently and, for this reason, cold-shouldered and finally beaten by its neighbors in World War I. Myth and blind surrender to a psychopathic leader could not stand the stark reality of total defeat. As by magic the German people turned away from their obsession and joined the ranks of freedom and democracy. But Communism is different. It is not founded on a myth or racial prejudice, but on an idea of freeing man from exploitation all over the world. This cannot be eradicated by force of arms but only through persuasion, nor could Communists, even after being defeated, be expected to turn to freedom under capitalism.

Others find a dialogue with Russians a waste of time. They may use the same words as we do, but they give them a totally different meaning and as a result one gets nowhere in a conversation with them. It is therefore better to let things take their course, since time seems to work to the free world's advantage. For after considerable initial gains which strengthened the Kremlin's belief that Communism is the wave of the future, and which were confirmed by their scientific successes, matters changed. While the Soviet Union was hard pressed in some vital economic sectors, Western Europe experienced unprecedented prosperity and

---

* Cf. Hans Kohn, "The Mind of Germany".

208

the United States' economy maintained a steady upward trend. The fact that forty per cent of the Soviet labor force cannot adequately feed the Russian people, whereas ten per cent of the American labor force produces a considerable surplus of food, throws a doubtful light on Soviet agricultural management. Moscow is no longer the undisputed leader of the Communist world and its relationship with Red China has reached the breaking point. The Kremlin's intervention in the Congo failed and so did its Cuba gamble, while some of the new African and Asian states which at first turned a willing ear to Soviet blandishments, are thinking better of it or have turned to China. The satellites are showing a new spirit of independence, and their loyalty becomes increasingly uncertain, should it ever come to war. Why then intervene instead of leaving things alone? The answer is that as long as the Cold War with its power complex and mutual suspicion lasts, the world is more at the mercy of an act of miscalculation or desperation than if a lasting element of rationalism can be introduced in our relationship with the Soviet Union. Moreover trends can change, for no nation of the free world is immune of economic depressions. The present aloofness of new nations towards Communism, motivated by the Hungarian tragedy, the Cuban affair, Moscow's contempt of the United Nations, China's war on India, etc. may one day be reversed to cooperation, should a forced industrialization "à la" Moscow or increased Communist foreign aid appeal to them.

The most important reason for talking to the Russians is that their decision to avoid nuclear war and seek further relaxation in no way guarantees an end to the Cold War unless they act from conviction instead of expediency. The Cold War can only be overcome if we add persuasion to our preparedness and determination.

If we let things drift, the endless recurrence of aborted negotiations and unallayed crises will make the average man of the West increasingly apathetic. The majority, preoccupied with their personal affairs, consider Communism rather as a threat to their welfare than as a movement incompatible with their convictions. It is this lack of awareness of the deeper challenge of Communism which can ultimately undermine the will to combat it. If free men become indifferent and seek to escape the global problem that confronts them, their horizon tends to become restricted, their foresight impaired, their creative thinking imperiled and their conscience stifled. They risk becoming increasingly narrow-minded, unable to find their innermost selves, isolated and incapable of rousing others to a common fight against the paralyzing effect of the Cold War. Their failure to recognize the Cold War for what it is, namely an effort to conquer free men by threats of impending disaster, makes them draw in their horns and succumb to their own weakness. They will end by cutting themselves loose from the spirit of our time, which demands that the individual think ahead and solve mankind's problems by a common effort. Even if nuclear war can be avoided, the fight against Communism must be continued by other means. For fight it we must to keep our self-respect and to safeguard man's freedom of thought. Only the nature of our arms must change, as the Communists discovered years ago when they started the war for men's minds. The greatest challenge our conflict with Communism poses is to our intelligence.

By conjuring up an image of man's evolution and formulating postulates for its further advance, the free world has an opportunity not only of correcting the shortcomings of the Communist creed but also of its own system. A nation unable to enter into a dispassionate dispute with an alien ideology lacks self-confidence and passes up a world-historic opportunity for serving the cause of freedom and of mankind.

At first the Russians may be reluctant to enter into conversations. Russia has not overcome the fear of encirclement by neighboring countries. This persecution mania is undoubtedly encouraged by their own strident anti-Western propaganda. Rumors are magnified and slight incidents distorted into proofs of their delusion. At times Russian aloofness and secrecy assume abnormal aspects. Such mass aberrations respond to treatment, in contrast to individual ones which are more difficult to cure. The treatment consists of establishing contact with the affected masses and offering them a more friendly projection of the presumed enemy.

The Dialogue Should Begin Now

The time to begin a dialogue is now. There are reasons in the West and the East against further delay. The West has once

210

again reached a turn in its history when its survival depends on gaining the initiative by an act of creative thinking. This is nothing new. At the beginning of its history, when periodically overrun by Goths, Vandals and Mongolians and forced into the defensive, the West had to use all its acumen to regain the lead. It succeeded in doing so with the invention of the compass, which gave it mastery over the oceans, improving its strategic position and permitting it to overcome and out-flank the hordes from the East. During the entire ensuing period war became the ultimate defense against invasions by foreign armies and ideologies. War was the last resort when reason failed. But since nuclear war has become unthinkable, the West has once more to regain the initiative for ending another kind of assault, this time of a subversive nature. Again the West has to fall back on its inventiveness. Should it, as in the past, produce a redeeming concept per-mitting the West to recover the lead, it will again influence the entire course of history.

There is a specific reason why it is the West which should take the initiative for conversing with the Russians. As these conversations have to be based on the evolutionary necessity to find a synthesis between freedom and collectivity, it is rather up to the country which throughout its history has been in search for a right equilibrium between individual and society than to one which purposely subordinates the individual to the collectivity. Without an intense social struggle and a constant urge to improve and renovate, the West could not have emerged as it is today, a world with a laboriously acquired but fair relationship between individual and com-munity. It is this slow and often painful process of adaptation between man and society with all the energy, thought and dogged struggle it required which qualifies the West to be the one to make the opening move. In order to follow the road to reason to its logical conclusion, the West must overcome its impatience with a "revolution" which failed to protect the individual from being pushed around, and attack the problem from a new, scientific angle in accordance with the direction of man's evolution.

The moment for a dialogue is also favorable on account of conditions prevailing in Russia. Communist leaders can no longer close their eyes to the "dementi" which history gives to the predictions of Marx and which reduces the propagandistic value of the Communist doctrine. The Russian masses, not to mention the satellite nations, are becoming restive under the influence of Western ideas which no Iron Curtain can stop. The younger Soviet generation is beginning to ask questions. It is no longer prepared to accept Marxist "truths" for the sole reason that the party upholds them. It has discovered pragmatism and wants to reach decisions of its own. A new wind is blowing over Russia's youth. Not yet a wind of freedom, but one of curiosity and scepticism. This is the natural reaction to the severe thought control exercised especially in art and literature. It may well occur to the men of the Kremlin that such a vacuum of disenchantment might usefully be filled by interesting the Russian people in the fascinating story of man's past and future as well as in an East-West cooperation in world problems.

The Inroads of American Thinking

Past experience with conversations between American and Russian scientists, researchers, businessmen and artists has been promising. The impact of American professors visiting Russia under the existing cultural exchange scheme was gratifying.

Especially American agricultural economists made a hit. Lectures as those by professor Leontief of Iowa State University about the input and output theory, or lectures about linear programming and machine solutions in agriculture as used in the U.S., impressed Soviet managers and technocrats, who derived some useful ideas from these capitalist concepts. There is no doubt that a field of scientific economics is being developed in Russia though it still may be called "application of mathematics to planning" in deference to Marxist dogma. A number of professors in other fields such as Harvard's Harold Berman, British philosopher A.J. Ayers and a number of others found attentive audiences. Their visits provided some Russians with a key to an hitherto hermetically closed door on self-inquiry. Such scientific exchanges help to foster creative thinking, something which has been restricted in the Soviet Union to such special fields as mathematics and exact sciences under the express condition that it does not impinge on fundamental Communist concepts concerning the course of history and the evolution of society. Visiting American

212

professors report about one hour lectures followed by three hours of discussion. This certainly offers an opportunity of planting some seeds, permitting us in the long run to introduce obliquely such subjects as the evolution of man.

In the course of the so-called Pugwash conferences, started in 1957 at the instigation of the American industrialist and self-styled friend of the Soviet Union, Cyrus Eaton, scores of American and Russian scientists such as MIT's Walt Rostov and Jerome Wiesner, CIT's Harrison Brown, John Hopkin's Bentley Glass, the University of Chicago's Leo Szilard and others met with such Russian scientists as Peter Kapitza, one of Khrushchev's close advisers, the late Alexander Topchiev, A.M. Kuzin and others as well as with numerous scientists from a dozen different countries, Britain, France, Austria, Poland, etc. During meetings that took place in the United States, Soviet Russia, and a number of European countries, discussions ranged from purely scientific subjects to studies on disarmament, combined East-West aid to underdeveloped countries, inspection systems under a general disarmament plan and other political problems. Though the political discussions did no more than clarify certain points of view, the participants found themselves often in agreement about problems arising from the latest breakthrough in science. It needs no effort of imagination to visualize the mutual advantage to be derived from a further comparison of experiences in physics, biology, medecine, space, etc.

In the satellites, interest in American thinking and scientific methods proved to be even greater, and the number of American scientific books translated into their respective languages is quite important. Because there freedom of discussion is greater, these countries are in a position to further advance an East-West scientific rapprochement. All this is encouragement for holding the kind of dialogue we have in mind.

How to Discuss Evolution

To draw Russian attention to the modern theory of evolution, either in scientific or private conversations, should not be overly difficult. Such conversations can best be initiated with commonsense approaches. In discussing, for instance, the present astronomical rise of state budgets, Americans can express the hope that our state expenditure of 20 billion dollars for project Apollo as well as our defense expenditure could be reduced, since no one in his right senses believes any more in nuclear war, and the money thus saved used for research, education and social services. Russians are likely to draw their own conclusions as to the significance of similar reductions in their own life. In a different approach, the need can be stressed for originality, and even eccentricity, without which a society becomes stagnant and cannot hope to survive, because the price of conformism is disintegration. Our Communist interlocutor may argue that Khrushchev has plenty of originality and eccentricity, and as long as he is the leader, this percolates down to the people. But in art and literature it is definitely not the case, and this prevents the individual from reaching his full potentialities and serving the collectivity as best he can. This aspect of the question may interest the Russians. Khrushchev once remarked in this connection that "the party is superior to their (i.e. the artists' and authors') consciences". He also said that "the will of the individual must be subordinated to the will of the collectivity", which implies that he recognizes the existence of collective conscience and a collective will. But then there must also be a world conscience and a world intelligence, which brings the conversation to one of the postulates of evolution. In this way various talks can be led in the desired direction.

Such indirect approaches facilitate discussion of the theory of evolution and its possible impact on the Cold War. Soviet Communists are likely to be interested in such philosophical abstractions. For deep down in his Slavic soul the Russian is a salvationist concerned with the fate of mankind. He might eagerly accept the conclusion that man has become an instrument of evolution, which heightens his responsibility for guiding mankind's destiny. As good chess player and strategist he is anxious to assume his share in influencing the destiny of the world. Communism is commonly regarded as atheistic. It remains to be seen whether the Russian Communist is not an agnostic rather than an unbeliever, and whether what he calls "the opiate of the people" is not a rejection of the institutionalized church rather than of religion. Communist leadership does not deny a Supreme Spirit as postulated by evolution. Evolution itself is not incompatible with dialectic materialism, which also seeks a rational explanation of the phenomena of life. Marx believed in Darwin's theory of evolution and equally in the possibility of progress. The fact that he chose his own way for achieving it does not preclude a discussion between Communists and non-Communists about the methods of furthering man's evolution. Marxism also accepts change. Though a totalitarian system is apt to freeze into dogma and avoid innovations as dangerous, Khrushchev made it clear that he recognizes change as a matter of course. His theory of co-existence is a case in point. Apart from this, Communists may be biased in favor of the theory of evolution, because they see it as a means to weaken the hold of the churches everywhere. But that is of secondary importance, the main thing being that Communism is not "a priori" opposed to a philosophy that deals with the universe in a rational way.* A concept which transcends the ideological deadlock and provides a way out of the Cold War may become acceptable to Russian scientific and managerial circles and even to party leaders.

When it comes to discussing evolution itself, it seems appropriate to acknowledge Russian understanding of the oneness of the masses all over the world, which other nations sometimes overlook in their preoccupation with national interests. Having made this point, a remark can be added about the creative powers of the individual, which constitute the other source of energy for mankind's continued evolution. Such an observation is not likely to fall on deaf ears, because Russians know that they need all the individual initiative and dedication they can get to succeed in their ambitious plans for catching up with the United States' economy. But a government which depends on creative individual forces has to concede the individual the right of having a will of his own, even though he has to subordinate it to the will of the whole. From here a conversation can branch out to a discussion of the fact that under a democracy the majority, and under Communism a small minority, is accepted as representing the will of the whole. The free world's attitude is based on the conviction

---

* A Russian translation of "The Phenomenon of Man" by Teilhard de Chardin was made under the auspices of the French Communist Senator Roger Garody, author of "Perspectives de l'Homme", in view of its distribution in the Soviet Union.

215

that to generate fully the individual's creative powers, he must be able to define spontaneously his political will, and that it needs the coordination of all creative powers for a society to keep up with the pace of modern progress. To a Communist rejoinder that Communism made headway with its system, the answer is that so did the free world. However, instead of talking about achievements, it might be more appropriate to dwell on shortcomings in both systems. In seeking to get at the root of these, both sides may find that they are caused by a too strong dependence on prevailing theory and lack of adaptation to the dominant force in life, which is change. In this way the conversation can revert to the theme of evolution and the obligations it imposes on mankind to fulfill its destiny.

Such talks can pave the way for later conversations on the diplomatic level. Khrushchev was a man capable of understanding the scope of the new theory of evolution. Taught by experience to distinguish between slogan and spirit and able to dedicate himself to a universal aim, he might have reacted to it in what for Communists is an unorthodox way. The same can be expected from at least one or the other of his successors whose outlook has inevitably been widened by their daily contact with him. The day must come that the United States and Soviet governments transcend the Cold War strife and grapple with the real problems of humanity. This means that the alternative is not coexistence or collision, and that the goal is not to win the Cold War. It means shifting from an artificially inflated ideological crisis, used as a means to gain power over the world instead of peace and prosperity for the world, to cooperation for solving mankind's difficulties. The population problem, the problem of conservation of the world's resources, of the creation of new sources of energy, of erosion, of poverty, of health, of education, of the transition from unskilled to skilled labor, of leisure, of exploration of space and sea, and above all of the study of man himself. To solve these problems other nations must join in the common effort which will help overcome the evolutionary crisis through which mankind is passing.

A New Purpose

From the moment that the U.S. is able to come forward with

a new world-encompassing purpose, everything will fall back into the right perspective. Remarks about a U.S. which, though having revolutionized political thinking and hoisted the flag of freedom, is unable to beat Communist propaganda, will be silenced. No longer will the peoples of the world protest if the U.S., discarding its self-restraint, declares that it will fight for what is right, for its fight will be based on a new lofty principle. The United States will again inspire the world and the Soviet Union will no longer be able to confuse the issues with high sounding but spurious proposals. In the end America's purpose may lift the entire world, Communists included, above the present senseless struggle.

The more ambitious and universal the tasks the U.S. proposes for cooperation, the more likely they are to attract Communist attention and to absorb energies which otherwise would be spent in arid doctrinaire pursuits, subversion or aggression. In their common effort to solve the concrete problems that endanger mankind, the United States and Soviet Union's dynamism will bring them nearer together and, imperceptibly at first, their views will begin to converge. Finally their cooperation will prove infinitely more interesting than their ideological strife. In an atmosphere in which reason prevails and the promise of a fabulous destiny is held out to mankind, power and prestige considerations lose their appeal and the world, freed from the spectre of mutual annihilation, can turn its attention to new challenges.

For it is not true, as some believe, that the Cuba experiment proved that not talking or cooperating but resolute action is the way to confront the Communist enemy. The United States' reaction to Cuba may have been the only attitude which a dictator understands and it may have served to outwit a dangerous power squeeze, it did not put an end to the use of force in America's intercourse with the Soviet Union. It hardly matters whether Moscow hoped to surprise the United States with a completed missile base in Cuba, or whether it intended to bait Washington into an invasion of Cuba, or for that matter whether by withdrawing from Cuba it could influence the U.S. to renounce the use of force in Berlin. It is equally immaterial whether Washington, which had to make a stand in Cuba, side-stepped the trap by instituting a blockade. What does matter is that both the Soviet attack and the American riposte stemmed from the same mentality of force, and that it is not through force or guile nor even by neutralizing the means of war, but only through rationalization and persuasion that the present world crisis can be overcome.

Political Realists Object

Political "realists" object that responsible statesmen cannot react to deeds or postures of aggression by words alone. They recommend the use of force, which is exactly what we reproach the enemy for doing. There remains the question of what to do in the case of Communist armed aggression. Should all other means of pressure and persuasion fail, then and only then must we oppose force by force. There is a great difference in having to resort to force because the enemy proves inaccessible to reason and in recommending the use of violence for overcoming Communism. *

The objection of the "realists" is wrong. This does not mean that if we can persuade the Russians the rest will be plain sailing. The end of the Cold War can but mean the end of one kind of crisis which will be succeeded by new crises of a different nature. If we harp on the need to end this crisis, it is because of its particularly dangerous nature resulting from the coincidence of man's inexperience with the deadly power he has acquired and his uncertainty springing from an as yet unassimilated scientific break- through. And if we insist that the United States must take the lead in extricating mankind from this specific crisis, it is because the U.S. is now in a position of leadership in which

---

* No wonder that violence evokes sympathy in the U.S. if one thinks of all the stories of violence daily served up by commercial television. Though the networks honestly attempt to raise the level of T.V., too many sponsors still insist on Westerns and murder stories. As government control of T.V. programs is incompatible with the American tradition, we will have to accept the bad with the good, because T.V.'s positive contribution outshines the harm it does to youngsters and others. Such a reserve is justified because the way to overcome these evils is not by direct action but by widening the understanding of people, reinforcing their independent judgment and intensifying their sense of re- sponsibility - in one word, by education.

it cannot afford to stick to emotional views and outdated methods of armed containment of ideological opponents.

At present there is a distinct effort of the main powers to steer clear of war, and what matters is keeping them going in that direction. Survival of mankind is more important than ideological differences, cooperation more precious than recriminations. The more contact and cooperation there is between capitalism and Communism, the greater the likelihood that they learn from each other. Tolerance is not only a moral imperative, it is also a commonsense requirement. If all energy consumed in fighting over differences were to be used for common efforts in a positive direction, mankind would be the beneficiary. Cooperation can even help opposed ideological systems to converge.

Chapter XIX

CONCLUSION

Any spiritual vision projected into practical politics is bound to appear anti-climatic. So slow are their day-by-day changes that only a glimpse can be caught of the goal which seems to remain as far removed as ever. What matters is the question: Are those changes going in the right direction?

In this respect there is no cause for doubt. Everywhere are signs pointing towards global oneness. The United States and other prosperous countries have taken the initiative of giving generous aid to underdeveloped countries. Western Europe, overcoming centuries-old traditions of national envy and enmity, has reached a large measure of economic integration. Of the members of the European Free Trade Association, Austria is about to join the Common Market, and the participation of Britain, the Scandinavian countries, Switzerland and Portugal can only be a matter of time. The Latin American nations are establishing closer relations within the framework of the Organization of American States. In the Middle East, Arab unity progresses. In Africa as well as in Asia, notwithstanding tribal wars and ideological disunity, many nations strive towards one or the other form of federation. Within the United States, the legislation for equal rights between the races is in the process of being slowly but surely enacted, and this bodes well for the future understanding of all races in the whole world. Finally, the two main opponents in the ideological struggle, the United States and the Soviet Union, are gradually but unmistakably drawing closer together. In the United States and other capitalist countries, the sense of collective responsibility in social matters has become so urgent, and in the Soviet Union and the satellite countries, mass education and standards of living have so much improved that the current suspicion against "creeping socialism" in the West is almost surpassed by the East's concern about "creeping capitalism". Apart from this, the determination of the two super-powers

Conclusion

to prevent nuclear war has created a common purpose in their foreign policy.

Under these developments, the Cold War has begun to recede. In due course, coexistence will become transformed into cooperation between the Soviet Union and the United States. This development, however, would present a great danger in a divided world where all major decisions could then be taken by the two super-powers alone. Therefore, the need for unity among the other nations becomes more and more urgent. If Europe is to assume its stabilizing and decisive role in world affairs, to which it is historically entitled, it must become not only economically integrated but firmly merged into a political entity. This example would compel the rest of the world to form, if not continental, then at least many-nationed federations.

In the course of such a logical development, it is likely that the countries of Western Europe would not stop at their economic and even political unification but come to some "de facto" agreement with Eastern Europe. This would clearly pave the way for the eventual integration of all Europe of which the Soviet Union is a geographical and historic part. Such a new Europe would automatically participate in every phase of global cooperation. This would permit all "haves" to make a coordinated effort to stop the ever widening gap between themselves and the "have-nots" and to reverse the present trend. Only then solutions to the most pressing problems of mankind would become possible. Contemporary man would at last be able to apply his newly acquired knowledge and technical skill to overcome poverty, hold down over-population, improve education and health everywhere, tap new resources of energy from the sea and the sun, preserve the world's resources, fight erosion, and make a concerted effort to explore space.

The technical feasibility of all this already exists. Its execution is delayed by man's inborn aversion against changes. This is a fact of life, and should be no reason for despair.

Looking back on recent events, an objective observer can reach the conclusion that contemporary man gave a fairly good account of himself. As a result of the development of his brainpower, he made remarkable advances in knowledge and technology. He did more. He did something which

221

hitherto had been considered impossible. Propelled into the greatest and fastest arms race in all history which, in terms of the past, would inevitably and unavoidably have led to total war, he was able to avoid war. With this achievement he finally entered the Age of Reason and performed the miracle of reversing a seemingly irreversible trend towards self-destruction, and with it the superiority of mind over blind fate.

From here on the road is open to recognize that in the future precedence must be given to the interests of mankind as a whole over and above considerations of national power and prestige. Ideological dogma must yield to reason, and the Science of Evolution that has just emerged will develop to provide the tools with which future generations and new statesmen may forge a world which, if not perfect, will at least be a place for wiser, less frightened, un-hating people to live and work together.

INDEX

Index